Life, Literature, and Thought Library

GODWIN AND THE AGE OF TRANSITION

LIFE, LITERATURE, AND THOUGHT LIBRARY

General Editor
PROFESSOR VIVIAN DE SOLA PINTO, D.PHIL.
PROFESSOR OF ENGLISH IN THE UNIVERSITY OF NOTTINGHAM

WILLIAM GODWIN
James Northcote
National Portrait Gallery

Godwin and the Age of Transition

EDITED BY
A. E. RODWAY

GEORGE G. HARRAP & CO. LTD
LONDON   TORONTO   WELLINGTON   SYDNEY

First published 1952
by GEORGE G. HARRAP & CO. LTD
182 High Holborn, London, W.C.1

*Composed in Garamond type and printed by
Western Printing Services Ltd, Bristol*

Made in Great Britain

FOREWORD

This series aims at presenting in an attractive form English texts which have not only intrinsic merit as literature, but which are also valuable as manifestations of the spirit of the age in which they were written. The plan was inspired by the desire to break away from the usual annotated edition of English classics and to provide a series of books illustrating some of the chief developments in English civilization since the Middle Ages. Each volume will have a substantial introduction, which will relate the author to the main currents of contemporary life and thought, and which will be an important part of the book. Notes, where given, will be brief, stimulating, and designed to encourage the spirit of research in the student. It is believed that these books will be of especial value to students in universities and in the upper forms of schools, and that they will also appeal very much to the general reader.

Grateful acknowledgment is made of the valuable help given to the series in its early stages by Mr S. E. Buckley.

VIVIAN DE SOLA PINTO
General Editor

PREFACE

GODWIN is among the smaller giants: those rather of an age than for all time. For that reason he is peculiarly important for an understanding of the spirit of the age; and, contrariwise, some knowledge of the age is necessary for a just understanding of the spirit of Godwin. His splendour and folly must be measured against the social and political background of a crucial period in our history. His influence, too, is conditioned by the political pressures of his period, which limited it almost entirely to literature.

Consequently, both Selections and Introduction are divided into three parts. The first is devoted to the background, the second to *Political Justice*, the great work springing from that background. The third, which includes selections from Godwin's own novels, gives specimens of the literary influence of that work. The total period covered extends from 1760 to 1830.

The limits of a book of this size have necessarily curtailed sections I and III of the text; they cannot pretend to give a complete picture or even to illustrate every point made in the Introduction. It is hoped, however, that they will give body to the spirit of that age by which *Political Justice* was provoked and on which it so provocatively impinged. "No work in our time," wrote Hazlitt, "gave such a blow to the philosophical mind of the country as the celebrated *Enquiry concerning Political Justice*. Tom Paine was considered for the time as a Tom Fool to him, Paley an old woman, Edmund Burke a flashy sophist. Truth, moral truth, it was supposed, had here taken up its abode; and these were the oracles of thought."

It is indeed by this one book that Godwin stands or falls.

Section II, the major section, therefore presents as nearly as possible, in an abbreviated form, the full range of Godwin's conceptions in *Political Justice*, and the corresponding part of the Introduction deals mainly with that work. The selections are taken from the third edition of 1798, not only on the critical principle of presenting the author's final version but also because it is impossible not to agree with Godwin himself in thinking it better, as a work of philosophy, than what he styled his first "crude and unequal performance."

Finally, the editor of this book wishes to acknowledge his indebtedness to the General Editor of the series, Professor V. de Sola Pinto, for the benefit of valuable advice at every stage of its compilation.

A. E. RODWAY

CONTENTS

INTRODUCTION

BACKGROUND

THE outline text-book of the eighteenth century commonly pictures the 'spirit of the age'—that volatile essence—as a movement from Augustanism or Reason at the beginning to Romanticism or Feeling at the end of the century: the two qualities being perpetually in inverse proportion, the one waning as the other waxes. Even for the second half of the century, when it becomes progressively less untrue, this is not the whole truth. For the first half it seems anything but the truth. Does Swift lack feeling? Is Young, of the satires on the one hand and *Night Thoughts* on the other, Augustan or Romantic? Do Pope's *Pastorals* show him to be a man of feeling? Or does his belief that "Whatever is, is right" mark him as a rationalist?

A truer, or at least a more useful, view sees the Augustan as an Age not of Reason but Compromise, whose chief virtues are prudence, tolerance, and politeness: one of those brief periods of stability when neither reason nor feeling is carried so far as to endanger the *status quo*.

After 1760, however, various latent conflicts become manifest, and the harmony of the era of Queen Anne gradually modulates into the Regency discord.

The seeds of discord are already sown, by the corrupt government of the Pelhams, at the time of Godwin's birth in 1756. They put forth shoots in the period of personal government by George III (1761–82), and come to fruition during the French Revolution and the English repression that followed it—during the period, that is, of Godwin's maturity.

As the old Augustan order becomes less and less satisfactory, provoking states of rebellion which tend to break it up, there is admittedly an ever greater increase in 'Feeling.' In religion, Methodism becomes the dominant force; in art, the Picturesque (the quaint or horrific) is added to the categories of the Sublime and the Beautiful; in literature, the period sees the rise of various types of primitivism (the admiration of societies less 'polite'), of sensibility, of horror, and of that untamed Nature which the Augustans had thought of, if at all, as 'horrid.' The great Romantics are the peak of this rise. It is not true, however, that there is a corresponding decline of 'Reason,' since the Utilitarians—at least as important in the early nineteenth century as the Romantics—are the peak of a similar rise.

There are, in fact, two ways of rebelling against an Age of Compromise. Such a period is not rational but reasonable, not passionate but moderate. Rebellion against it will, therefore, be rationalistic and passionate—the rebels being both natural allies and natural antagonists.

The antithesis of 'Reason' and 'Feeling,' then, is over-simple. Its inadequacy is seen unmistakably at the end of our period, when the various strands are clearly defined. Arctic Utilitarians and torrid Romantics, after Waterloo, are equally opponents of that stubborn Augustanism which lingered on into the new century to oppose innovation, whether literary or political.

During the period of Godwin's maturity, then, there are at least three diverse schools—Rationalist, Romantic, and Conservative—each containing several classes. Their relationship, moreover, is not one of simple antagonism. Byron, a Romantic, admires the arch-augustan, Pope, and attacks Southey and Wordsworth. Prosecutions of radicals are often initiated not by the Conservative Government but by the Society for the Suppression of Vice, headed by Wilberforce, the reformer. Moreover, the Rationalists' creed is related to Romantic unreason by its basis of *faith* (in, for instance, the natural rights of man, or the rational hedonist). The Romantics' emotional rebellion, on the other hand, is based on intellectual theories, whether metaphysical (as for Blake, Wordsworth, and Coleridge) or political (as for Shelley and Byron) or literary (as for Keats). For both emotion and theory are prerequisites of rebellion. Without theory emotion is intermittent and ineffective. Without emotion theory is sterile.

Nevertheless, when all proper allowance has been made for variation within each category it is not possible to place Godwin in any: the elements are too closely and evenly combined. Indeed, his peculiar interest and significance lies in the fact that he *contains* the complexity of a disordered and disintegrating age.

The Augustan era was perhaps, by its very nature, bound to disintegrate. It insisted on freedom of thought, person, commerce, and invention, and at the same time on institutional immutability. Consequently, the country outgrew its institutions, and free intelligences became critical. None the less, the inevitable was accelerated by the determination of George III to reign as an active king. Lack of a Tory party strong enough to be independent, to keep both Whigs and Crown in check; the custom of government by corruption; and the £12,000 out of the Civil List set aside by the King at every general election to buy votes for Government candidates opposing the Whig aristocrats—all these enabled him to govern for twenty years through a hired Cabinet of 'the King's Friends.'

At the beginning of that period England was prosperous and stable, respected in France as a power, and admired as a land of freedom and philosophy. At the end she had lost America and was friendless in Europe, while at home men were becoming increasingly aware of anomalies and abuses, increasingly interested in the theory and practice of political morality.

Not that the King's government was necessarily worse than any other would have been. In the Gordon riots, for instance, the King displayed an energy and initiative completely absent from Parliament or City Council. But, by being unorthodox, it drew attention to its shortcomings.

Nor were anomalies and abuses necessarily more numerous than before, nor the gap between rich and poor of greater consequence. But changing circumstances were rendering these things more noticeable. Enclosures and agricultural improvement, the Industrial Revolution and the new roads and canals that facilitated it, the growth of commerce connected with the overseas markets of the new Empire: these factors were changing more than the face of England. They were changing its spirit.

That twenty-year period brought sharply to notice how ill-adapted to changed conditions was the Tudor machinery of government, how remote from control a Parliament whose members had first bought votes and now sold them.

Corruption was not, of course, entirely selfish. Newcastle, that master of ministerial 'management,' left public life £300,000 poorer than he entered it. But what a noble family might lose in government could be recovered from the Church. At the close of the century the Manners's held eight English and twelve Irish sees, one member of the family, with many pluralities, drawing some £650,000 from the Church. Watson, Bishop of Llandaff, lived practically all his life at Windermere, yet held a chair at Cambridge and fourteen livings in Huntingdonshire, Shropshire, and Leicestershire. Nor could it be said in mitigation that quality was high in State or Church. Walpole's accounts of "the burlesque Duke of Newcastle" are well known; and of Dr Blackbourne he wrote "This jolly old archbishop of York had the manners of a man of quality, and though he had been a buccaneer and was a clergyman, he retained nothing of his former profession except his seraglio." None the less, he was rumoured to keep Dick Turpin as his butler!

Such, at least, was the view which presented itself most clearly. The compensations—the patronage that the wealthy and the Government extended, by means of grants or sinecures, to men of letters and science, the disinterested learning of many churchmen, and their lack of fanaticism—were virtues by their nature unobtrusive. Whereas no one could help noticing, for instance, the contrast between the tepidness of diocesan work and the zeal with which the same clergy in the courts and the House of Lords supported a succession of repressive Criminal and Game Laws, and gave effect to hundreds of Enclosure Acts.

The rapid increase of enclosures, after 1760, was an in-separable part of that progress in farming methods which enabled England to feed her growing population—a population, even so, that could not have been supported without the equally unpopular new inventions which ushered in the industrial era. In each case, however, the manner of their introduction and the uncontrolled results caused widespread discontent. The poor man deprived of his rights of common and his share in the village lands obviously lost. The enclosing landlord, whose large-scale modern methods might increase his rent-roll tenfold, obviously gained. So, too, with the mill-owner and the mill-hand. The hand, working fourteen hours a day, or longer, and starving when mills closed down in a crisis of overproduction, contrasted his life with that of the owner, working when he chose, living well, and offering visitors their pick of the mill-girls.

Again, the benefits were indirect and therefore overlooked, though in fact the industrial hand at the end of the eighteenth century seems to have worked shorter hours and to have fed better than the home weaver at the beginning of it. But if poor men were less poor the middle classes and the aristocracy were disproportionately more wealthy.

The widening gap between them was due mainly to a rapid increase of population—among the causes being not only

B

improved medical science, and the reduction of fever that went with the draining of newly enclosed land, but also the improved standard of living from industrialization. The increase, however, of itself kept the standard of the many *comparatively* low. It meant that, despite the increase of industry and commerce and the cultivation of formerly uncultivable lands, there was always a labour surplus; and, therefore, wages were never very high. Consequently, workers were not compensated by them for the loss of commons and village industries. For the middle-class investor, on the other hand, this was the Golden Age, since expansion created a demand for capital. England was rapidly becoming divided into Disraeli's "two nations," whose ideas and culture were as different as their incomes.

The division was psychological too. The agricultural labourer was no longer hired by the year and boarded with the farmer. He was now kept at a proper distance. For the independence of a share in the common lands of the village was substituted the dependence of a two-roomed cottage and a weekly wage; the cottage being a device to discourage him from going to the town. The industrial worker, also, was more remote from his middle-class *nouveau riche* employer than his father from the aristocrat on whose estate he had lived. At least he had been solicited and 'treated' during elections. Not so his son. Owing to the shift of population during the Industrial Revolution, from the south-east to the north-west, the newly built and thickly populated areas of the towns were outside the franchise area and returned no members. The old, and often depopulated, boroughs still returned their previous quota. Before the Reform Bill of 1832 Old Sarum returned two members although without a single voter. At Gratton Sir Mark Wood owned all six houses, paid the rates and taxes, and was therefore the sole voter. In contrast, Glasgow had only thirty-three voters in a population of two hundred thousand. The Church was in every way as corrupt as the Government, and the pocket borough was paralleled by the pocket benefice, where there was neither church nor congregation. Ecclesiastical corruption, however, aroused far less agitation in England. In the countryside the tithe-paying farmer regarded the clergy as his natural allies against the nascent socialism of the miserably paid agricultural proletariat. The new towns, lacking new churches, were not disturbed by old corruption. The workers, moreover, found consolation in enthusiastic Methodism; and under the influence of Methodism the Church began to reform itself. By 1790 nearly 500 clergy supported Wesley, where only six or seven had done so in 1750.

For this reason the Whig reform movement, that started immediately George III began to exploit the established abuses for his own ends, remained purely political, apart from a small Dissent element. Led by Burke, the Whigs demanded administrative reform, and, when the King was forced to drop the reins of government after the loss of America, the brief Rockingham Government did in fact diminish abuses—though as late as 1800, twenty years after Rockingham's purge, it was estimated that £1,500,000 were paid out yearly in sinecures.

The Radicalism of the period, however, whether Romantic after the fashion of Blake or Rationalist (and influenced by French anticlericalism) after that of Paine or Godwin, was deist or atheist, or at least highly unorthodox, and attacked abuses not only in law and government but also in the Church. Indeed, it regarded those three pillars of society as an unholy triumvirate, in which each supported the others.

Radicalism on these lines accelerated steadily after 1760, receiving impetus from the disruption of the old order, from the concentration of workers in the factory districts, which made easier the spread of Radical organizations and propaganda, and from the focusing effect of such propaganda. The misery of an apprentice in an attic might go unnoticed or be regarded as exceptional, but not the misery of the 30,000 children of Lancashire who worked, in 1795, a fourteen-hour day, whipped into wakefulness, and none the less often maimed by the machines as they dropped asleep on their feet. Old Sarum might go unchallenged, but not when contrasted with unenfranchized Birmingham.

With the growth of discontent and the disruption of the old structure of society came increased lawlessness, and in reaction an increased severity in the law. In the second half of the century capital offences increased from 160 to 253, death being the penalty for theft over 5s. (or 1s. by pocket-picking). Of this aspect of the period, which Godwin inveighed against in persistent horror, Samuel Rogers gives a chance glimpse:

> When I was a lad, I recollect seeing a whole cartful of young girls, in dresses of various colours, on their way to be executed at Tyburn. They had all been condemned, on one indictment, for having been concerned in (that is, perhaps, for having been spectators of) the burning of some houses during Lord George Gordon's riots. It was quite horrible.
>
> Greville was present at one of the trials consequent on those riots and heard several boys condemned, to their own excessive amazement, to be hanged.
>
> "Never," said Greville, with great *naïveté*, "did I see boys *cry* so."[1]

Such a background gave fervour to the idealism of reformers like Godwin. But against it must be set not only material improvement, but also the growth of humanitarianism and sensibility that accompanied it. Social brutalities were considerably curbed, and the way was paved for wider reforms. Lord Cobham may have been crude enough to spit in Lord Herevey's hat for a bet, but an unamused society punished him with the nickname 'Lord Gob'em' or 'Spitter' ever afterwards. Hellfire clubs were becoming less numerous. Brutal sports, it is true, still existed. There were still bull-baiting, women's boxing, sparrow-biting (trying to bite off the head of a clipped sparrow fluttering in the crown of a hat), and goose-riding

[1] *Recollections of the Table Talk of Samuel Rogers*, edited by A. Dyce (1856).

(attempting to snatch off the head of a tied goose with greased neck). But these and similar sports were declining, as Godwin grew up, under the pressure of a distaste he shared. Agitation arose, particularly in the 1780's, on behalf of slaves, prisoners, and paupers—the latter being particularly hard hit at this time by a sharp rise in prices: the quartern loaf, for instance, having risen by 1795 from 3d. to 1s. Up to 15 per cent. of the population were receiving some form of parish relief; and the custom of allowing contractors to tour the countryside with gangs of workhouse children aggravated unemployment.

But reform seemed imminent, and in fact under Rockingham, and later Pitt, the eighties saw much improvement. Corruption was reduced, the Cabinet system established, finances reconstituted, and a new Empire founded on the ruins of the old. But the monopoly of power by the landowners remained, and when in 1789 the French Revolution broke out it was used rigorously to defend the *status quo* against any encroachment of democracy, against anything which might disturb the balance of the Constitution between King, Lords, and Commons. Thomas Hardy, in 1794, was tried for treason, having advocated "representative government, the direct opposite of that which is established here."

The reform movement had come to a full stop. Not unnaturally, for the Revolution had crystallized Radical discontent, given it a catchword theory, and an example of action. In such a crisis, the Tory Government felt obliged— by the lack of police and the possibility of revolution—to adopt drastic measures.

The reaction of the Tory Party, however, though natural enough, seriously aggravated the social and economic ills attendant on the Industrial Revolution which was all the time proceeding. Romantic and rationalist Radicals joined in demanding a new order. The Tories were forced to acquire for the first time a coherent, though not a scientific, philosophy formulated mainly by Burke, who had moved to the right as the threat to the *status quo* changed from Jacobite to Jacobin. When this philosophy was countered by Paine's *Rights of Man* (1792) the alliance of the two contrasting schools of revolt was aptly symbolized in that warning by Blake which enabled Paine to flee the country before arrest.[1]

The "two nations" were in effect at war—a cold war embittered by thwarted hopes, by repression, and by the heavy taxation which followed the outbreak of war with France in 1793. The landowner throve on enhanced rents, the merchant tended to benefit because Continental shipping was kept off the seas, but the indirect taxation which mainly financed the war pressed on the poor. Though prices rose, action to obtain corresponding wage increases was prevented by legislation forbidding trade unions. And this was but part of a general repression: Habeas Corpus was repealed, public meetings banned, the freedom of the press abolished, the penalties for seditious writing increased, the anonymous publication of newspapers prohibited. Those prosecuted by the Government were not allowed to prove the facts alleged and could be tried by a 'special' jury. Magistrates were empowered to inflict the death penalty.

In contrast, penal laws against Catholics were allowed to lapse or were repealed, Methodists were explicitly sanctioned by law, and freedom of religious association was respected. In fact, considerable deference was shown towards religion. In 1798 the Lord Chancellor refused to hold any more dinners on the Sabbath. In 1805 Wilberforce persuaded Parliament to stop Sunday drilling. In 1809 Spencer Perceval, the new Prime Minister, ceased to call Parliament on Monday so that members should not be tempted to travel on the Sabbath. In 1818 Parliament voted £1,000,000 for church building. For, after all, most shades of religion could be assumed to be opposed to the atheistic Jacobinism of the *Philosophes* and their English followers.

---

[1] He was sentenced to death in his absence.

Among these followers was William Godwin, then a man of thirty-six, formerly a Dissenting minister, and now in 1793 feverishly writing *Political Justice*, sending the first books to press before the later ones were written, in order that Radical enthusiasm might be guided into proper channels. Tried by immutable criteria, the present state of affairs was found wanting, and one all-embracing system gave the remedy, a remedy based on the eighteenth-century assumption that man is a rational being.

For all the sensation it caused, it can be clearly seen that *An Enquiry concerning Political Justice* is very much of its period—in what it is *for* as in what it is *against*. The concept of perfectibility, for instance, springs from the evident material improvements of the age, and is closely associated with contemporary theories of evolution which were supplanting the static Augustan concept of man and the universe.[1] Condemnation is not felt to be inconsistent with perfectibility. If men distribute the profits of improvement wrongly the fault is not inherent in them but a result of their institutions, which blind them to the Good. The anarchism is obviously related to the Government's many sins of omission and commission, and it has an economic counterpart in the Free Trade agitation of the Utilitarians. Similarly, Godwin's looking forward to the life of simplicity is a counterpart of the romantic 'Back to Nature' movement, of which Rousseau was the chief advocate. The suggestions on education and the law carry to a logical conclusion ideas which had occurred not only to the *Philosophes*

[1] The Augustans saw the universe as a 'Great Chain of Being': the necessary expression of God's creativity. Nothing, therefore, could be altered or omitted: a doctrine leading to deist religion and political inertia. It contains the paradoxical consequence that apparent evil must be considered actual good. To get rid of the paradox, and also to account for the fact of Change, the Chain must be temporalized, shown as Goodness and Creativity *becoming* perfect in time rather than *being* perfect in space. This leads to romantic religion and reformist politics, and to the evolutionary theory of men like Lamarck in France and Erasmus Darwin in England—to say nothing of the Scot, Monboddo, so satirized by Peacock for suggesting that men were descended from ape-like ancestors.

(Helvetius, d'Holbach, Mably, Diderot) but also to moderate humanitarian reformers in England—to whom, indeed, Godwin is more nearly akin in this respect. In his attack on riches he significantly dwells as much on ostentation as on economics—the very natural reaction of a sometime Dissenting preacher to that *noblesse oblige* which clad Selwyn's acquaintances in five-hundred-guinea suits, or cost the Duke of Norfolk £70,000 at play in one night.

Even Godwin's aberrations, behind their logical façade, often have an empirical origin. Who can doubt, for instance, when he argues against salaries for the civil servants of his Utopia, that at the back of his mind lurks a memory of eighteenth-century sinecures? Indeed, two of his main concepts, Reason and Necessity, both have roots in the French and English speculation which followed Locke in trying to achieve in the moral and political worlds what Newton had achieved in the physical.

The attempt to find simple laws to explain men's behaviour, in much the same way as the behaviour of the planets could be explained, involved abandoning the doctrine of innate ideas. Man must start as a blank, a body at rest. Thereafter, what he experiences will explain what he is. Sensations from the outer world, transmitted to the brain, will give rise to simple ideas. By association—a psychological 'law of gravity' —simple ideas will be combined into complex ones. In the moral sphere, too, there is a gravitational law, the 'law of Reason' (or 'Nature'), which holds the moral universe together. (Hume is almost alone in maintaining that "Reason is . . . the slave of the passions.") Sociological theory—which culminates in Utilitarianism—is inevitably hedonistic and determinist. If man starts as a blank then he is what he is by virtue of necessity. Having no innate moral ideas, his social morality will also be determined (on the pleasure-pain principle). Assessment of probable pleasure or pain in given circumstances will be made by his reason. Only 'enlightenment' therefore is necessary in order that he should act morally: that is, in such a way that his action would produce in society—of which he is a part—a greater sum of pleasure than of pain.

In short, doctrines *akin* to those of Godwin are properties of the age. It was left to him to transmute them into a creed capable of firing two generations of poets—while the original doctrines hardened into the utilitarian calculus. What gave *Political Justice* its power was its union of cool reason and glowing faith. Godwin is, as it were, a Utilitarian in his rational method and terminology, but a Romantic in so far as he is an emotional rebel, turning religious fervour into materialistic channels.

But Godwin was the crest of the toppling wave. After him the shattered, though victorious, rebellion against the old order was no longer that of the whole man. Reason and Feeling became ever more separate, the Utilitarians denying the latter, the Romantics abjuring the former. The one led to blue-bookery, to gradgrinding bureaucracy, the other to a religiosity that Godwin would equally have deplored.

GODWIN

IF Godwin's was part of a general social revolt, affecting politics, arts, and speculation alike, the question still remains why, or rather how, did it come to take its particular form?

Two major influences are at once apparent: his early life and his later reading. Together they account for his being able to fuse in one book two divergent strains of revolt.

Godwin's upbringing affected the rest of his career, despite the fact that he early abandoned the Sandemanians—that sect which "after Calvin had damned ninety-nine in a hundred of mankind, has contrived a scheme for damning ninety-nine in a hundred of the followers of Calvin." It is not, however, the simple effect of his having received fervour and faith from his early religion, and reason and materialism from his later reading. There is the double complication of a strong rational element in his religious education and an element of rebellion in his nature. At the fine liberal Dissenting academy at Hoxton, which he attended from 1773 to 1777, every one else was an ardent Whig; Godwin chose to be the sole Tory. He was also the sole 'Sandemanian'[1]; nevertheless he is to be found in his last year taking the negative side in a 'paper war' on the existence of God.

Furthermore, there is the influence of his development to consider. During the six years after leaving Hoxton—for much of which he was a preacher—Godwin passed through several stages of Dissenting thought, each one influencing him both directly, and, as he ceased to believe in it, by reaction. After reading Priestley, he adopted Socinianism, the doctrine that denies the divinity of Christ, having previously moved to a more orthodox Calvinism than Sandeman's. After meeting Holcroft, he became an agnostic; a debt he repaid by converting Holcroft into one of the most fervent antagonists of the prevailing order.

In this complex of experience can be found the origin of most of Godwin's characteristic tenets, and it is difficult not to think his reading rather a result than a cause of them—especially as his many fundamental divergences from the authorities, mentioned in footnotes to *Political Justice*, seem generally to be conditioned by his former beliefs. The very intention of the work as stated in his diary seems, in its unworldliness, rather religious than sociological:

> In the first fervour of my enthusiasm I entertained the vain imagination of "hewing a stone from the rock" which, by its inherent energy and weight, should overbear and annihilate all opposition, and place the principles of politics on an immovable basis.

In the book itself there is much evidence that the manner of Godwin's revolt was influenced by Dissenting theory.

[1] An extremist Dissenting sect, whose members were admitted by a "holy kiss" and believed in community of property.

That theory was far from homogeneous. Practically the only point on which all shades of English Dissent agreed was hostility to State control and the right, indeed the duty, of private judgment. Here, Godwin is clearly in the Dissenting tradition; there can be little doubt that his firmness on this point and his readiness to suffer martyrdom derive from it. But Godwin is essentially a moralist. For him political, legal, and economic problems are fundamentally problems of morality. Here he is not so clearly in the Dissenting tradition, for the Dissent doctrine of election, since it leads easily to antinomianism,[1] is not essentially moral. If a man is saved not by Works but by Grace, it is but a short step to considering the natural order of morality unimportant, the spiritual order all-important.

There are, however, three ways of avoiding antinomianism while still retaining freedom of private judgment. The first, that of such Dissenting Platonists as Price, is to postulate eternal truths, which are apprehended by the individual reason. The second, that of rational Whig Dissenters like Toulmin and Kippis (the head of the Hoxton academy), is to accept the doctrine of 'natural law,' intuitively self-evident. The third, that of Socinian Dissenters like Priestley, is to accept the laws of associationist psychology. Godwin uses all three methods of escape, appealing now to absolute truth, now to an equally absolute reason, now to the laws of the human mind as a basis for morality.

Thus, something of his rationalistic argument, as well as much of his idealism is traceable to his varied connexions with English Dissent. Other causes, of course, may contribute. Part of Godwin's fervent championship of independence and tolerance is no doubt due to reaction against the severity and fanaticism of a father he disliked. There is also the influence of a reaction against the Dissenting tradition itself. There is to be

[1] The doctrine that the moral law is not binding on Christians under the "law of grace."

no Godwinian Elect. All men are morally equal and are entitled to the same treatment. Truth is to be arrived at by the slow process of reason, the continual practice of sincerity and free discussion, not by a sudden access of Grace. The millenium is to be earthly not heavenly. Moreover, the majority of Dissenters, chiefly as a result of the Test Acts, thought in terms of politics. They favoured associations for the purposes of repeal, and looked to legislative action for social reforms. Godwin objected to associations, as a denial of independence and a substitution of group pressure for the force of truth; and he distrusted political solutions of what were for him moral problems.

On the whole, then, the emotional bases of Godwin's thought are largely the result of his Dissenting upbringing; the rational superstructure is largely the result of reaction from religious conclusions—though the *rational* Dissenting strain affects the method of his reaction.

The fervent beliefs: in liberty, equality, justice, non-violence, in the power of truth, and in the doctrine of complete candour —these derive directly or indirectly from some branch of Dissenting Christianity. The premises from which he demonstrates the need for, and the arguments by which he shows the inevitable results of, those principles derive more usually from materialist philosophy.

The two main premises he borrows are the doctrine of Necessity and the pleasure-pain evaluation of goodness. In both cases, however, Godwin departs from his authorities. Firstly, although his phrasing is reminiscent of the *Système de la Nature*, he rejects d'Holbach's pure materialism, and admits the human will as part of necessity. Involuntary actions in the past are materially determined, but voluntary actions are determined by a judgment of the future. Moreover, enlightenment, by making the mind more fully conscious, makes the area of possible involuntary action ever smaller. As the enlightened mind necessarily chooses the good (since evil is merely error springing from lack of knowledge) necessity is in practice hardly distinguishable from free will, the will to be enlightened. In this way Godwin attempts to unite in one system scientific predictability and moral choice. Secondly, he includes altruism and the feeling of rectitude among the pleasures. Indeed he insists that the pursuit of virtue is the highest pleasure—and the virtue pursued is an absolute not, as for the *Philosophes*, a relative good. Pleasure, in fact, becomes a by-product of the pursuit of other values. In particular, Godwin values highly sincerity and individuality, both of which are subordinate in Helvetius and Mably to utility.

It is in thus allowing what may be shortly called idealism that Godwin differs most strikingly from Bentham. It enables him to abandon the political and religious 'sanctions' by which the latter would keep order, and thereby to abandon government, retaining only the moral sanction—the force of public opinion.

In this manner the gap is bridged between Godwin's life and reading.

His inferences naturally differ from those of the *Philosophes* or such English Radicals as Paine and Thelwall. The doctrine of perfectibility (that is, the possibility of continual *improvement*) leads to gradualism not revolution. He believes in lessening and finally abandoning government. The *Philosophes* believe in improving and increasing it. They believe that man is guided by self-interest and is, therefore, to be governed by punishment and reward. Godwin believes him to be fundamentally a social creature (rendered selfish by government) who can therefore be guided, when free, by the dictates of justice, which he will discover through his own enlightened judgment. Where they stress the rights of man Godwin stresses his duties. A right implies something we may choose to exercise or not. But justice requires that we should always act morally. We have, therefore, no positive rights, only the negative right of freedom to become what we are capable of becoming, and the *claim* that others should act morally towards us as we towards them.

The moralistic basis of Godwin is well shown by a comparison of his view of political institutions with that in Helvetius, or that of his chief source, Burke's *Vindication of Natural Society* (1756). Helvetius seeks the failure of monarchy in the faulty character of most monarchs. Godwin thinks it inherent in its bases of inequality and imposture. Burke's *Vindication*, like *Political Justice*, considers the three systems of government—monarchy, aristocracy, and democracy, and shows that all are bad, but does not take monarchy to depend on a lying assumption of natural inequality. Moreover, Burke's presumably ironic conclusion is that we should "vindicate ourselves into perfect liberty"—that is, into chaotic anarchy. Implicit is the suggestion that we should make the best of the present system. Godwin, on the other hand, will not accept an immoral system merely on the ground that its impostures are useful. The democratic government of checks and balances of power must, therefore, give way slowly not to anarchy but to a form of democracy in which moral self-government will make other government unnecessary.

This belief in man's perfectibility Godwin held to the end, despite the long years of calumny and hatred, when former admirers showed the genuineness of their recantations by joining the attack; despite, too, the longer years of oblivion.

Indeed, all the main contentions of *Political Justice* remain in principle unchanged through the three editions of 1793, 1796, and 1798. Barely one month after Paine had been sentenced to death for *The Rights of Man* Godwin sent to press that preface to the first edition which ended, with typical calm confidence:

... but exclusively of this precarious and unimportant consideration [*i.e.*, the author's safety] it is the fortune of the present work to appear before a public that is panic struck, and impressed with the most dreadful apprehensions of such doctrines as are here delivered. All the prejudices of the human mind are in arms against it. But it is the property of truth to be fearless and to prove victorious over every adversary. It requires no great degree of fortitude to look with indifference on the false fire of the moment and to see the calm period which will succeed.

To that attitude Godwin remained faithful, though it was not without risk. As late as 1813 he was charged in a State Paper[1] with teaching pernicious ideas to the young through the sinister school primers that were then his sole means of support: an absurd charge that was never pressed. In 1793 he had escaped a similar charge only because Pitt—unprepared for pirated editions and working men's group-subscriptions—thought that "a three-guinea book could never do much harm among those who had not three shillings to spare."

There is, admittedly, considerable revision in the later editions, but its object and effect is simply to introduce superior clarity and system into the first "crude and unequal performance." There is no warrant for De Quincey's charge of recantation against the second edition, nor for the myth of timidity that has sprung from it.

Godwin contends, briefly, that "the happiness of the human species is the most desirable object of human science to promote." Intellectual and moral happiness is preferred. Such happiness never has been the general lot, but man's progress shows that it could be in the future—but only by introducing universal political justice. For man's intellectual and moral characteristics, unlike his physical constitution, are the result not of heredity but environment. By 'justice' Godwin means an imperative reciprocal morality:

If it be just that I should confer a benefit, it is just that another man should receive it, and if I withhold from him that to which

[1] Domestic George III, 1813 (January to March) No. 217.

he is entitled he may justly complain. And what is just between individuals is just for society as a whole, since "society is nothing more than an aggregation of individuals."

How, then, are men to be brought to such a pitch of benevolence that they will give away whatever they do not need themselves to whomever needs it? Obviously not by the stick and carrot of the *Philosophes*, but by the enlightened reason. Reason is not here opposed to feeling; it must in fact be aided by a virtuous disposition, a sensitive conscience. With such aid it inevitably reigns over the senses. If it did not, future progress towards justice would be impossible, since there can be no enlightenment of the senses.

From these contentions it follows that government must be abandoned. For it rules not by reason but by compulsion, and therefore, far from aiding man to scale the heights of truth it actually prevents his doing so. It prevents the disintegration of error before the power of truth. Force, moreover, implicitly denies moral equality. All men are able to be just, and all are entitled to justice, to equal reward and pleasure in life: government perpetuates injustice and inequality.

Punishment is similarly to be condemned for hindering progress by setting force above enlightenment. In rare cases, where immediate physical harm is possible, the criminal may be imprisoned, but his punishment should be as light as possible, and combined with an effort to awaken his reason to the principles of benevolence. Law necessarily shares this condemnation. For one thing it attempts to make permanent what men—or rather the set of men in power—at present perceive of the eternal laws of moral justice. But if perfectibility is true men's understanding will improve; from age to age they will see more deeply into the nature of justice, and the law will always be out of date—yet law relies on precedent! Furthermore, it judges for, and against, others instead of allowing to each the exercise of his own unaided judgement. The law judges by broad categories and takes account only of results, whereas justice assesses each case individually and is concerned mainly with motives.[1] Finally, law as a branch of government relies not on justice but force. Yet law may be completely at variance with morality. Is it just then that it should be enforced?

National education, too, is suspect, for its quality, and as an organ of the State. A very natural suspicion for one accustomed to the contrast between the excellence of the independent Dissenting academies of the century and the licensed torpor of Oxford and Cambridge.

The moral imperative inherent in Godwin's conception of justice disposes also of promises, oaths, and contracts, including the contract of marriage. The nature of morality requires us always to do what is just: so that, binding us to what is or what becomes unjust, they are immoral; binding us to what is just, superfluous—and evil in so far as they substitute a form of compulsion for an independent moral judgment. The vote too is condemned because it assumes truth to be in numbers, and implies that minorities may be coerced.

But what are Godwin's positive contributions towards the millenium? Firstly, plain-spoken sincerity is essential if error and injustice are to be vanquished. They are founded on opinion, on the support of some or all people, and when opinion is changed they will fall. Secondly (and this is Godwin's major contribution to practical political science) he advocates a gradual decentralization, and, as men become enlightened, a withdrawing of authority, legal and administrative. Eventually the force of public opinion alone, in a small and candid community, will be sufficient to restrain and reform the evil-doer. Thirdly, all wars must be abandoned, except those to repel an invader (for which purpose some centralization is permissible). Lastly, the institution of property is to be placed "upon an equitable basis."

---

[1] In the second edition Godwin distinguishes between virtue of the agent, depending on motives, and virtue of the act, depending on results.

C

Godwin speaks avowedly as a moralist concerned with the principles of possession, not as an economist concerned with the practice of supply and demand. Justice dictates that an article of property belongs "to him who most wants it, or to whom the possession of it will be most beneficial." He has not a right to take it, but the possessor has a duty to give it. For his own use he is entitled to keep only a subsistence plus whatever of his production is not needed for another's subsistence.

Equality of property will, on the one hand, free men from envy, servility, and truckling. By assuring necessities for the body it will assure independence of mind. On the other hand, the rich will be freed from corrupting flattery, laziness, ostentation, and satiety. Instead they will possess "the cheerfulness that arises from industry perpetually employed about objects of which our judgment acknowledges the intrinsic value." Moreover, under such a system "all occasions of crime would be cut for ever." An immense intellectual gain would result, since the equal sharing of labour, together with the banishing of superfluity and the improvement of machines, would enormously increase man's leisure. The progress of enlightenment and benevolence would be an accelerating one, since each stage would automatically create more favourable conditions for the next.

For the first difficult stages Godwin relies confidently on the powers of reason. Show men what must be done to benefit mankind, and as their judgments appreciate the justice of one's argument they will do it. This is not *possible*: by the twin doctrines of Necessity and the Omnipotence of Truth it is *inevitable*.

At this point a bald exposition reveals the main flaw of *Political Justice*, a flaw camouflaged in the book itself by Godwin's consummate argument, by the obvious sincerity with which he searches out all possible objections, and answers them, not merely with abstract logic but also by example. Given

his assumptions, indeed, one can make only minor criticisms
of his argument. It is the assumptions that are questionable.

In particular, Godwin's belief in the dominance of reason
seems, to this century at least, psychologically unreal. Who
can take seriously, for instance, Godwin's answer to the
objection that with the abolition of want the earth would
become overpopulated?

> Reasonable men then [*i.e.*, in the age of Justice] will propagate
> their species, not because a certain sensible pleasure is annexed
> to this action, but because it is right that the species should be
> propagated, and the manner in which they exercise this function
> will be regulated by the dictates of reason and duty.

The same unreasonable rationalism, in his own person,
leads him to pronounce against gratitude and personal or
family affections, as examples of non-universal, *ir*-rational (and
therefore 'un-Godwinian') benevolence. It leads him to
disapprove all too logically of the white lie to spare pain, or the
deception to save one's life from unjust men. He fails to see
that what is logically desirable may be psychologically im-
practicable. Moreover, too much reason means not enough
common sense. Hence, for example, Godwin argues from
abstract principles that unsalaried public servants would *not*
"pay themselves by ways a thousand times more injurious."
Common sense should have convinced him to the contrary.
Nor does he perceive that his scheme for supporting those
public servants who are not independent by the voluntary
action of the wealthy leads straight to that parliamentary
corruption he detested in contemporary England. Again, he is
led to condemn the ballot as injurious to openness and firmness
of character—blind to the fact that only so can the unbiased
judgment he desires be exercised, since fear, whether it should
or not, in fact often will overcome judgment.

The revisions of the later editions, however, tend to correct
this fault, to humanize Godwinism—a tendency the later

novels and essays carry farther, though never so far as to alter its main contentions.

The attack on marriage is modified, by removing the discussion on surnames and uncertainty of paternity, and by directing the offensive more specifically against the 'present system': a system inextricably bound up with property and contracts. Godwin's brief and happy union with Mary Wollstonecraft has produced a genuine change of outlook. Again, the third edition allows somewhat more importance to heredity, admitting that "children certainly bring into the world with them a part of the character of their parents." Passages dealing with private and domestic affections undergo superficial modification. For Fénelon's chambermaid who might be my "wife or mother" (and "a fool or a prostitute") is substituted a valet who might be my "brother or father" (and "a fool or a profligate"). The rational obligation to save Fénelon remains.

The most important change—the first sign of an increasing realism in Godwin's outlook—is in the greater weight given to feeling in general, in the "Summary of Principles," which was prefixed when the third edition was in the press. The Summary goes beyond the text. Godwin's notebook[1] for the same year goes beyond the Summary:

> As every man will know more of his kindred than strangers so he will inevitably think of them oftener, feel for them more acutely, and be more anxious about their welfare. This propensity is as general as the propensity we feel to prefer the consideration of our own welfare to that of any other human being. Kept within due bounds, it is scarcely an object of moral censure. The benefits that we can confer upon the world are few, at the same time that they are in their nature, either petty in their moment, or questionable in their results. The benefits we can confer upon those with whom we are closely connected are of great

[1] Data for an intended book, *First Principles of Morals* ; *i.e.*, Godwin meant to modify his views publicly. (Further detail is given in Woodcock's *William Godwin* (see Bibliography).)

magnitude, or continued occurrence. It is impossible that we should be continually thinking of the whole world, or not to confer a smile or a kindness but as we are prompted to it by some abstract principle of philanthropy.

For all that, the doctrine of universal benevolence is not abandoned. Benevolence begins at home but is not to stop there.

This humanizing movement is not ended by the death of Mary Wollstonecraft, nor by the unprincipled attacks on Godwin and his dead wife, nor even by the disastrous second marriage with Mrs Clairmont (1801), which, by saddling him with a petty and wasteful woman and two—soon to be three— children in addition to Fanny Imlay and Godwin's own daughter, condemned him to hackwork for the rest of his life. *Fleetwood* (1805) and *St Leon* (1799) expressly modify the doctrines of *Political Justice* by extolling marriage and the domestic affections. *St Leon* too goes so far as to state that the chief attraction of children is their individuality. Having children of his own has modified Godwin's views just as marriage did. In *Thoughts on Man* (1831) he even concedes innate moral dispositions, and is thereby constrained to reverse the earlier rôles of Reason and Education—in order to avoid the conservative conclusion that men are born to be for ever good or bad.

By this time Godwin's faith in reason was chastened. He was seventy-five, and ill, and had suffered thirty years of irrational abuse: from Government supporters for being a revolutionary, and from Radicals for not being one. The French Revolution had failed to establish liberty, yet Europe was still seething with revolution. At home were riots, mob-risings, rick-burning. Political and legislative measures, rather than moral ones, were hoped for by reformers. It was hard to believe in the power of the individual reason or the omnipotence of truth. "We pretend," he wrote, "to have each of us a judgment of our own; but in truth we wait with the most patient docility, till he whom we regard as the leader of the chorus gives us the signal."

In keeping with this trend, the third edition of *Political Justice* changes the motive of voluntary action from "the idea of certain consequences" of an event to "the hope or fear of that event." The change from an idea to an emotion is slight but significant. In *Thoughts occasioned by Dr Parr's Spital Sermon* (1801) Godwin writes:

> Without feeling we cannot act at all; and without passion we cannot act greatly. But when we proceed to ascertain whether our actions are entitled to the name of virtue, this can only be done by examining their effects, by bringing them to a standard, and comparing them with a criterion.

Here Reason is emotive but still the dominant factor in choice. By the time of *Thoughts on Man* imagination has replaced reason as the instrument of reform. There is a new emphasis on "sudden and irresistible conviction."

In the same way, the seed of feeling allowed to virtue in 1798 ("kind and sympathetic feelings, reduced into principle" —*i.e.*, turned by reason into rational universal benevolence) has blossomed into a doctrine of spontaneity and abnegation. Virtuous actions arise from "an exalted point of self-oblivion" reached by love.

It is difficult to believe that the changing climate of opinion has not influenced Godwin's movement from unfeeling reason to reasonable feeling. Not that he has become affiliated to the first of the two dominant movements of the new century, Romanticism and Utilitarianism. He still unites qualities divided between them. Rather, something of his early beliefs has been unconsciously resuscitated in a disguised form; for this is also the age of Religion. With the French Revolution eighteenth-century rationalism of all kinds had become suspect. Even Dissenting religion, if rational, must lead to atheism and rebellion, and on to hell. Consequently the rational Presbyterian and Unitarian sects declined, while sects flourished whose emphasis on Grace and spontaneous conversion recalled the Sandemanianism of Godwin's youth.

Throughout all the changes, however, the fundamental principles of *Political Justice* persist. The novels written to illustrate them, and the essays to develop or amend them, proclaim the same convictions: the duty of private judgment, the right of free speculation, the objection to imposture or inequality, the rejection of egotism and force, the belief in human benevolence, the teleological argument for perfectibility, the vision of what man may become if he choose. They are perhaps neither true to psychological fact nor founded on "an immovable basis" of logic; but, through the quality of the writer's mind—comprehensive, self-critical, forbearing, disinterested—and set forth in a style of compelling energy and clarity, they gave to their own troubled age a coherent and humane idealism sadly lacking in ours.

INFLUENCE

The general pattern of Godwin's influence in his lifetime is clear. There were three periods: of Fame, Attack, and Oblivion.

The first was a brief period of popularity and happiness. The publication of *Political Justice* brought not only fame but also the admiration of a number of intelligent and beautiful women, including Mrs Inchbald, the actress and novelist, Amelia Alderson, the belle of Norwich, Maria Reveley, and 'Perdita' Robinson, the famous Shakespearean actress, friend of Coleridge and author of twenty-seven volumes of prose and poetry. Her experiences as mistress of the Prince Regent (who deserted her, and defaulted on a bond of £20,000) inclined her towards Godwin's views on royalty—and not only on personal grounds. She had seen it from the inside, had worked with Fox and Sheridan, for instance, in their largely unsuccessful efforts to prevent the Duke of Cumberland from ruining the Prince by dissipation and debauchery, in order to spite the King.

Most of this circle, indeed, held some at least of Godwin's views. Mary Hays, a novelist, believed in the equality of women and proposed to Godwin, who rejected her. Her main importance lies in the fact that she later furthered the association of Godwin and Mary Wollstonecraft, the noble and gifted writer of *A Vindication of the Rights of Woman*, and persuaded her to marry him when she was about to have a child. Mary herself, despite her bitter experience with the American, Imlay, who left her in Paris with a baby, was still in principle opposed to marriage, as was Godwin. Their legal union was therefore kept as secret as possible, and they continued to keep separate, though neighbouring, dwellings and to live as far as they could rather as man and mistress than husband and wife.

Mary's death in childbirth, in 1797, coincided with a change of public opinion. To Holcroft, Godwin wrote with just foreboding, "I firmly believe that there does not exist her equal in the world. I know from experience that we were formed to make each other happy. I have not the least expectation that I can now ever know happiness again."

Shortly afterwards one of his most brilliant allies, Mackintosh, publicly reviled Godwin and recanted his beliefs. As Porson maliciously put it, he "meant to have Interest on his Principle." Nor was he the only one. Even Thelwall, whose life he had saved by his pamphlet of 1794, began to vilify him (though for reasons opposite to those of Mackintosh).

That pamphlet stands out even in the brilliant first period which produced *Political Justice*; *Caleb Williams*, his one good novel; and the essays of *The Enquirer*.

In the autumn of 1793 five Radicals in Scotland (where the law favoured the chance of a satisfactory verdict) were tried by the Government for the treasonable activity of attending a Convention to discuss shorter parliaments and universal

suffrage. They were sentenced to fourteen years' imprisonment, from which four never returned. With this success
behind it, the Government extended the attack to England.
On May 12, 1794, Thomas Hardy, the shoemaker who founded
the London Corresponding Society, was arrested, and within
a few days ten others, including Horne Tooke and Thelwall,
were detained on the same charge. Holcroft, when the charge
was presented in October, gave himself up to stand trial with
his colleagues.

The charge was cleverly and elaborately worded to give
the impression that the accused had been plotting the over-
throw of the Government. Godwin's keen logical brain had
little difficulty in seeing that in fact it boiled down to an
unprovable assertion that, though the acts of the accused were
not treasonable, their intention was, and therefore their acts
might become so. An assertion remorselessly demolished: " An
association for Parliamentary reform may desert its object and
become guilty of High Treason. True; so may a card club, a
bench of justice, or even a Cabinet Council."

After a detailed refutation of the charge, Godwin ended with
an eloquent attack that could well have hanged him:

> The Chief Justice quits in this instance the character of
> criminal judge and civil magistrate, and assumes that of natural
> philosopher, or experimental anatomist. He is willing to dissect
> the persons that shall be brought before him, the better to ascer-
> tain the truth or falsehood of his preconceived conjectures. The
> plain English of his recommendation is this. Let these men be
> put on trial for their lives; let them and their friends be exposed to
> all the anxieties incident to so uncertain and fearful a condition;
> let them be exposed to ignominy, to obloquy, to the partialities
> (as it may happen) of a prejudiced Judge and the perverseness of
> an ignorant jury; we shall then know how we ought to conceive
> of similar cases.

It was, as Hazlitt described it, "one of the most acute and
seasonable political pamphlets that ever appeared," and

probably not only saved the lives of the defendants but also saved England from an oppression as rigorous as those on the Continent a generation later.

To the period of fame succeeded a period of parody and satire from all quarters, during which Godwin wrote his *Memoirs of the Author of a Vindication of the Rights of Women*, a moving account which sufficiently dispels the legend that Godwin was icily inhuman; *St Leon*, whose heroine was modelled on his dead wife; a reply to Dr Parr's attack on him; and a life of Chaucer.

When that period ended, about 1804, the reaction had submerged Godwin. Shelley was astonished some years later to find that he was still alive. The next period, of oblivion and hackwork, produced nothing likely to add to Godwin's reputation; the chief fount of Godwinism was Shelley.

At no time before his death in 1836 had Godwin any noticeable effect on either politics or justice. The measures passed in the seventeen-nineties, reinforced in 1817, and extended in 1819 inevitably prevented the spread of non-violent Godwinism,[1] not only by their repressive and effective action but also by the rebellion they provoked. Not candour but underground societies and treasonable plots, not gradualism but armed riots and insurrections—these were the order of the day. Indeed, violent revolution seemed almost inevitable in the period of distress and high prices after 1815. Several factors, however, prevented it. There was the opening of new markets and a renewal of trade; the reaction at Thistlewood's conspiracy to assassinate the whole Cabinet at dinner; the royalist turn given to popular feeling when the Queen, during her grotesque trial for adultery, identified herself with the cause of freedom, in opposition to the King and Ministers. Above all, there was the conservative effect of revived religion,

---

[1] I avoid the term 'anarchism' because, although Godwin's voluntary self-regulating communities are anarchist in the modern sense of the word, he himself takes 'anarchy' to be equivalent to 'chaos,' and of course condemns it.

which offered adequate heavenly compensation for earthly injustice, and an outlet for dangerous emotion. By 1820 the current of reform was flowing safely in parliamentary channels, and the repression gradually eased, but by that time Godwin and Godwinism were forgotten. The Whigs were regaining their former position as liberal leaders, and much of their theory was provided by Utilitarianism, which was neither revolutionary nor anarchist. The reign was beginning not of moralists but of the economists and calculators prophesied by Burke—then a conservative, but, none the less, significantly admired by Godwin.

For all that, Godwin had a delayed and indirect effect on affairs after his death, mainly through his early influence on Coleridge, Owen, and Francis Place. Through Owen and Place Godwinism affected the Trade Unions and the Co-operative Movement, and thence the temper of English Socialism. Place and Owen sought a solution rather through independent workers' associations than through governmental direction: a solution directly contrasting with the authoritarian solutions offered by the Jacobins and the Chartists. A few individual Socialists like William Morris and George Bernard Shaw[1] reveal a more direct influence. Oscar Wilde, indeed, adopts—and adapts for Art's sake—most of the Godwinian creed in *The Soul of Man under Socialism*.

In Godwin's day, however, the influence of *Political Justice* was necessarily confined to literature. His own novels, avowedly written to popularize his message, have as their constant theme the lone individual's conflict with the overwhelming organization of society. They possess the qualities to be expected from a man of Godwin's ability. They want nothing but life. The intense, lucid Latinized style, so admirable for works of exposition, makes his novels curiously disembodied and intellectual. The creative artist's gift for vivid

[1] Compare *Back to Methuselah* with Godwin's speculative appendix on *The Prolongation of Human Life*.

image and evocative phrase is missing. Moreover, Godwin found it painfully easy to express himself. In consequence his characters rarely converse; they harangue each other. The heroine of *Fleetwood*, for instance, incredibly takes five and a half pages to say 'yes' to a proposal of marriage, from a man both rich and beloved. Yet, with all admissions made, *Caleb Williams* remains one of the best novels of the period. It is shorter than Godwin's later works, and it conveys its message more through action, less through adumbration. Not that it can be said to portray, as the secondary title has it, *Things as They are*. On the contrary, it is often fantastic. But the implacable pursuit does express—at rare intervals with almost Kafkan fascination—the symbolic experience of life under 'a reign of terror.'

The reason for the failure of parodists is clear in the novels after *Caleb Williams*. They *are* parodies; enlarging all its faults and diminishing its virtues. In a passage in the early part of *Fleetwood* Godwin shows critical insight:

> All these things live in my memory and constitute a picture which will never be obliterated while this heart continues to beat. But I suppress these circumstances at the risk of rendering my narrative flat and repulsive by its generalities.

The risk is only too real.

Nevertheless, these novels are no worse than the productions of Holcroft, Mrs Inchbald, Mrs Robinson, and other Radicals who wrote Godwinian plays and novels. The *inspiration* of *Political Justice* is found in the poets—though, at best, it shows as a general fertilizing effect. Where the poets are more undilutedly Godwinian, as will be seen from some of the selections, they tend to be less inspired.

Wordsworth, Coleridge, and Southey all idolized Godwin in their revolutionary youth. The Pantisocratic[1] scheme of the last two is pure Godwinism, and the same heady creed is

---

[1] Pantisocracy (Greek: 'all of equal power'). A communistic Utopian society intended to be founded on Godwin's model by the Susquehanna River.

evident throughout their early poetry, usually in heretical incompleteness. Wordsworth, according to Hazlitt, told a chemistry student to burn his "books of chemistry and read Godwin on necessity." Despite this, it is difficult to say what Wordsworth got from Godwin. *Descriptive Sketches*, written before *Political Justice* was published, contains such Godwinian lines as those on the child of Nature who

> Walk'd none restraining, and by none restrain'd,
> Confessed no law but what his reason taught,
> Did all he wish'd and wish'd but what he ought.

The Godwinism attacked in *The Borderers* would not have been recognized by Godwin, for Oswald, the supposedly Godwinian mouthpiece, by his selfishness, his deceit, and his advocacy of violence and murder, violates the chief canons of Godwinism; while the attacks on war, monarchy, and the penal code in the published version of *Guilt and Sorrow* are common radical themes. The earlier manuscript versions, however, both in their matter and in their rather more abstract treatment show a more definitely Godwinian influence.[1] But what most deeply and permanently affected Wordsworth was probably rather the idealistic detachment than the philosophical doctrines of *Political Justice*.

Certainly, Wordsworth, together with Coleridge and Southey, abjured those doctrines after the disillusionment of 1798, when Napoleon invaded Switzerland, a free republic, and thus ceased to be the 'liberator.'

After that date there appeared only parody and satire, until 1811, when Shelley heard with "inconceivable emotion" that Godwin was not yet "enrolled in the list of the honourable dead." In 1814 Shelley eloped to the Continent with Mary Godwin, daughter of Mary Wollstonecraft and, later, author of *Frankenstein*, the Godwinian story of a monster made wicked by society's treatment of it. They were accompanied by the

[1] For details of these versions see de Selincourt's *Wordsworth's Poetical Works*, Vol. I.

daughter of Godwin's second wife, Jane (Claire) Clairmont, who later became Byron's mistress.

The outcome of the association was disastrous. Claire conceived the unfortunate child Allegra by Byron. Harriet, Shelley's wife, apparently pregnant by a lover who had deserted her, drowned herself in the Serpentine, in 1816. Godwin was reported to have sold Mary and Claire for £800 and £700 respectively, and the scandal cost Fanny Imlay, his other step-daughter, her post as a teacher. In her devotion to Godwin she poisoned herself rather than add to the burden of his poverty.

It is scarcely surprising that Godwin condemned Shelley. Nor it it so inconsistent as critics have maintained. Though he discountenanced marriage, Godwin would not have dreamed of suggesting that sexual attractions should blind the attracted to the general good. Certainly the good of Godwin, his wife, Fanny Imlay, Harriet, and (as it happened) Claire was not furthered. Nor were Mary and Shelley acting in accordance with the Godwinian principle of complete candour by their clandestine meetings and stealthy departure.

Their marriage in 1816, however, reconciled Godwin, and may well stand as a symbol of the creative union of God-winism with Shelley's poetry.

After meeting Godwin, Shelley reread *Political Justice* in 1812, 1814, 1816, 1817, and 1820 at least. He was therefore familiar with all editions. Further, the Godwin he met had moved away from his first extreme rationalist materialism. This is in keeping with Shelley's transition from the revolutionary materialism of *Queen Mab* (most of which was probably written under the influence of the first edition) to the Platonic idealism of his later poems. Again, Godwin's non-human 'principle of the universe' is not far removed from the Demogorgon of *Prometheus Unbound*; and Shelley's Intellectual Beauty could be taken as a counterpart of Rational Benevolence.

None the less, it would be an exaggeration to say with Brailsford "that Godwin formed Shelley's mind, and that

Prometheus Unbound and *Hellas* were the greatest of Godwin's works." Undoubtedly Godwin's was an immense and a lasting influence. Even in 1820—a period of great embitterment owing to Godwin's demands, not for more money than Shelley felt himself morally bound to give, but for more money than he could spare—Shelley wrote:

> You will see
> That which was Godwin, greater none than he;
> Though fallen—and fallen on evil times—to stand
> Among the spirits of our age and land
> Before the dread tribunal of *to come*
> The foremost—while rebuke cowers pale and dumb.
>
> LETTER TO MARIA GISBORNE

Shelley, indeed, was born to be Godwin's disciple. His style has the same disembodied energy, the same metaphysical rather than physical texture; and they shared the same qualities of mind: extreme independence, disinterested enthusiasm, and impassioned intellectuality.

Yet even to *Queen Mab*, with its fascinating and voluminous footnotes to enforce the Godwinian message, Shelley brings ideas of his own. The belief in the taming effect of vegetarian diet, for instance, puts material before moral causes. Romantic love is not one of Godwin's pleas in the argument against marriage, nor is the "*impulse* of unerring Nature" a Godwinian justification for adultery, or anything else.

This, indeed, is a permanent divergence. Though neither is impressed by the marriage system, Godwin thinks that vows and legal fetters are making too much of what is in fact trivial; whereas for Shelley passion is almost holy, the union of lovers a type of the union of all things in the *One*, and interference is sacrilege.

Here we approach the main difference from Godwin. After 1815 or 1816 Shelley is greatly influenced by Plato, and his development is the story of a struggle to unite two philosophies—the one materialist, the other idealist—and thereby to find a *motive* for Godwin's secular altruism. It is found eventually in a semi-religious, semi-platonic conception of Nature.

In *Queen Mab* Shelley had mainly adopted Godwin's conception of Nature as law or Necessity. This leads to the dilemma that the institutions that make man evil are just as 'inevitable' as his final emancipation. Godwin is hardly aware of the difficulty (that material Nature—and the less material nature of man—may just as probably be innately evil as good). Shelley develops a conception of Nature as a Spirit of Love, which he seems to identify with a Platonic *One* unifying the *Many*.

There is an attempt to fit this conception to materialism: the *Many* is unified by the *physical* rhythm and order of "the one *Spirit's* plastic stress." Thus the Good is wedded to the Necessary. None the less, it is not a purely rational and secular idea. Realization of this, perhaps, caused Shelley to attempt to reconcile rationalism and religion in the *Essay on Christianity*.

He there maintains that there is a "principle which unifies the universe, the overruling Spirit of the collective energy of the moral and material world." It is called God, but is the same thing as, or at least works through, the laws of Nature. Necessity and the Spirit of Love are thus reconciled. The following are perhaps the key passages:

> God, it has been asserted, was contemplated by Jesus Christ as every poet and every philosopher must have contemplated that mysterious principle. He considered that venerable word to express the overruling spirit of the collective energy of the moral and material world. He affirms therefore no more than a simple sincere mind is the indispensible requisite of true science and true happiness. He affirms that a being of pure and gentle habits will not fail, in every thought, in every object of every thought to be aware of benignant visitings from the invisible energies by which he is surrounded. [Here is Godwin's Benevolence explained by being given a semi-religious origin.]

> Whosoever is free from the contamination of luxury and licence, may go forth to the fields and to the woods, inhaling joyous renovation from the breath of spring, or catching from the

odours and sounds of Autumn some diviner mood of sweetest sadness, which improves the softened heart. . . .

We are not the arbiters of every motion of our own complicated natures; we are not the masters of our own imaginations and moods of mental being. There is a Power by which we are surrounded, like the atmosphere in which some motionless lyre is suspended, which visits with its breath our silent chords at will.

That is, we are creatures of Necessity, which, while it may be a 'Spirit of Love,' is also 'the law of Nature' merely. We cannot therefore assert that there is a Providence guiding us. Pictures of future Paradise, whether in life or after it, must be considered an ideal, not a reality: "We see God, and we see that he is good. How delightful a picture, even if it be not true." The two contradictory concepts of Nature are welded, in fact, by making Nature into God, while at the same time making God into Nature.

Symptomatic of this *attempted* resolution of conflict are: the transmutation of Godwin's 'benevolence as a means' to Shelley's 'love as an end'; the greater emphasis on "the empire of feeling"; the vision, in *Prometheus Unbound*, of man's future undividedness, when passion and reason are one (Passion being, as it were, Nature-as-Love; Reason, Nature-as-Necessity); and finally, the emphasis on the need for a change of heart so that this union can come about. This will happen when man is in harmony with Nature where the union is already effected. Such union gives a *spiritual* power analogous to the colder *rational* non-violence of Godwin. It is as poetry to prose:[1]

> To suffer woes which Hope thinks infinite;
> To forgive wrongs darker than death or night;
> To defy Power which seems omnipotent;
> To love and bear; to hope till Hope creates
> From its own wreck the thing it contemplates;

[1] From *Prometheus Unbound*, by P. B. Shelley, *l.* 570.

D

> Neither to change, nor falter, nor repent;
> This, like thy glory, Titan, is to be
> Good, great and joyous, beautiful and free;
> This is alone Life, Joy, Empire, and Victory.

What Shelley has done with Godwin's doctrine of non-violence is typical. As he developed, Godwin's principles remained the basic elements of his thought, but were transmuted into his own substance. Resolving idealistically the main paradox of Godwinism, Shelley more and more infused feeling into the creed, generalized the ideas, and raised them to the plane of poetry, expressing them less as a philosophy, than as a vision, of life as it is and as it might be.

Nevertheless, Godwin remained the dominant influence in his poetry from *Queen Mab* at the beginning, through *The Revolt of Islam* and *Prometheus Unbound*, to the *Masque of Anarchy* and *Hellas* at the end. Moreover, contrary to popular belief, his was a restraining influence, for Shelley had a tendency to be far more actively and aggressively revolutionary than Godwin. (Witness the latter's letter of 1812, urging Shelley to rely on free discussion rather than on organizing the Irish to fight for Catholic Emancipation.) In Shelley's poetry the *Ode to Naples* and the violently toned passage prudently omitted by his publisher from *Hellas* are evidence of the tendency.[1]

Apart from Shelley's poetry, the influence of Godwin, during his last period, is clear only in Peacock's satire and some of the early novels of Bulwer Lytton, Godwin's last disciple. But it is glimpsed elsewhere in a line or a chance phrase; and imperceptibly it helped to create the optimistic libertarian individualism of the Victorians.

---

[1] "This is the age of the war of the oppressed against the oppressors, and every one of those ringleaders of the privileged gangs of murderers and swindlers, called Sovereigns, look to each other for aid against the common enemy, and suspend their mutual jealousies in the presence of a mightier fear. . . . But a new race has arisen throughout Europe nursed in the abhorrence of the opinions which are its chains, and she will continue to produce fresh generations to accomplish that destiny which tyrants foresee and dread."

I. LIFE AND THOUGHT

STANDARDS OF LIVING

RURAL POVERTY

Poor, yet industrious, modest, quiet, neat,
Such claim compassion in a night like this,
And have a friend in every feeling heart.
Warmed, while it lasts, by labour all day long
They brave the season, and yet find at eve,
Ill-clad and fed but sparely, time to cool.
The frugal housewife trembles when she lights
Her scanty stock of brushwood, blazing clear,
But dying soon, like all terrestrial joys.
The few small embers left she nurses well;
And while her infant race with outspread hands
And crowded knees sit cowering o'er the sparks,
Retires, content to quake, so they be warmed.
The man feels least, as more inured than she
To winter, and the current in his veins
More briskly moved by his severer toil;
Yet he too finds his distress in theirs.
The taper soon extinguished, which I saw
Dangled along at the cold finger's end
Just when the day declined, and the brown loaf
Lodged on the shelf, half eaten, without sauce
Of savoury cheese, or butter costlier still;
Sleep seems their only refuge: for alas!
Where penury is felt the thought is chained,
And sweet colloquial pleasures are but few.
With all this thrift they thrive not. All the care

Ingenious parsimony takes but just
Saves the old inventory, bed, and stool,
Skillet and old carved chest, from public sale.
They live, and live without extorted alms
From grudging hands, but other boast have none
To soothe their honest pride that scorns to beg,
Nor comfort else but in their mutual love.

WILLIAM COWPER, *The Task* (1783)

THE FRUGAL BOARD

The Hostess opes the willing door,
And then recounts the humble store

Which her poor cottage could afford to place upon the frugal
board.
The home-spun napkin soon was laid, the table all its ware
displayed;

The well-broiled rasher then appeared,
And with fresh eggs his stomach cheered;
The crusty pie with apples lined
Sweetened the feast on which he dined,

And liquor that was brewed at home, among the rest was seen
to foam.

WILLIAM COMBE, *Dr Syntax in Search of the Picturesque* (1809)

A SCANT SUPPER AND NORMAL BREAKFAST

. . . But Syntax look'd to satisfy his palate rather than his eye,
And that eye was disposed to stare when it beheld the bill of
fare.

One dish a single pigeon grac'd,
On t'other side three larks were plac'd;

A tart, about two inches square, cut out and fashioned like a
star,

Potatoes two, most nicely roasted
The produce which her garden boasted,

And in the midst the eye to please, a milk-white Lilliputian
   cheese
Were all arranged in order due and were so pretty to the view.

      The Doctor who so long had fasted,
      Nor since 'twas noon a morsel tasted,

Besides he had kicked down his tea beheld this festive symmetry

      Decked out in all the simple cost
      That Wedgwood's pottery could boast,

In hungry fury almost able with the scant meal to eat the table.

When in due time refreshed and gay he hail'd the promise of the
   day,
And in the bookroom was display'd the luxury of breakfast
   laid.
His eyes now joyous wandered o'er the contrast of the night
   before:
The tea in fragrant fumes ascends, the sister coffee too attends,

      While many a smoking cake appears
      In butter soused o'er head and ears;
      Boil'd eggs, sliced beef and dainty chicken
      Invite him to more solid picking,

While honey of delicious taste adds sweetness to the morn's
   repast.
   WILLIAM COMBE, *Tour of Dr Syntax in Search of a Wife* (1810)

CORRUPTION

ELECTIONS

Launceston Election results:

    Hon. Mr Rawdon and Mr Brogden   12 votes.
    Dalkieth and Garthshore   11 votes.

The contest was a hard fought duel between the Duke of

Northumberland and the Duke of Buccleuch. Both parties
have spent a great deal of money; but the former has carried
the day.

Shrewsbury Election. The State of the Poll on Monday was
Sir W. Pulteney, 1607; John Hill Esq., 834, Hon. W. Hill, 832.
The Election will cost Sir Richard Hill £100,000 at least;
the Expense to each party is about £1000 per day.

The Times (1796)

MINISTERIAL CORRUPTION

When Grafton shook Oppression's iron rod,
Like Egypt's lice, the instrument of God;
When Camden, driven from his office, saw
The last weak efforts of expiring law;
When Bute, the regulator of the State,
Preferred the vicious, to supplant the great;
When rank corruption through all orders ran,
And infamy united Sawney's clan . . .[1]
Deep in the secret Barrington and Gower,
Raised upon villainy, aspire to power;
Big with importance, they presume to rise
Above a minister they must despise;
Whilst Barrington, as secretary, shows
How many pensions paid his blood and blows.
And Gower, the humbler creature of the two,
Has only future prospects in his view
But North requires assistance from the great,
To work another button in the state . . .
Some system of economy, to save
Another million for another knave;
Some plan to make a duty, large before,
Additionally great, to grind the poor:

[1] *I.e.*, the Earl of Bute's.

For 'tis a maxim with the guiding wise,
Just as the commons sink, the rich arise.
If ministers and privy-council knaves
Would rest contented with their being slaves,
And not with anxious infamy pursue
Those measures which will fetter others too,
The swelling cry of liberty would rest,
Nor Englishmen complain, nor knaves protest.
But courtiers have a littleness of mind,
And, once enslaved, would fetter all mankind . . .
Whilst Wilkes to every Briton's right appealed,
With loss of liberty that right he sealed.

THOMAS CHATTERTON, *Resignation* (1770)

THE FUTURE

This truth of old was Sorrow's friend,
'Times at the worst will surely mend':
The difficulty's then to know
How long Oppression's clock can go;
When Britain's sons may cease to sigh,
And hope that their redemption's nigh.

When vile Corruption's brazen face
At council-board shall take her place,
And lords and commoners resort
To welcome her at Britain's court;
Look up, ye Britons! cease to sigh
For your redemption draweth nigh.

When civil-power shall snore at ease,
While soldiers fire—to keep the peace;
When murders sanctuary find,
And petticoats can Justice blind;
Look up, etc.

Commerce o'er bondage will prevail,
Free as the wind that fills her sail;
When she complains of vile restraint
And power is deaf to her complaint
Look up, etc.

When tax is laid, to save debate,
By prudent ministers of state;
And what the people did not give
Is levied by prerogative;
Look up, etc.

When popish bishops dare to claim
Authority in George's name;
By treason's hand set up, in spite
Of George's title, William's right;
Look up, etc.

When George shall condescend to hear
The modest suit, the humble prayer;
A Prince to purpled pride unknown!
No favourites disgrace the throne!
Look up, etc.

When time shall bring your wish about,
Or seven-years lease, *you sold*, is out,
No future contract to fulfil;
Your tenants holding at your will;
Raise up your heads! your right demand!
For your redemption's in your hand.

THOMAS CHATTERTON, *The Prophecy* (1770)

TAXATION

TAXING THE ENGLISH

Should foreigners staring at English taxation,
Ask why we still reckon ourselves a free nation,
We'll tell 'em we pay for the light of the sun,
For a horse with a saddle, to trot or to run;
For writing our names; for the flash of a gun;
For the flame of a candle to cheer the dark night;
For the hole in the house if it lets in the light;
For births, weddings, and deaths, for our selling and buying;
Tho' some think 'tis hard to pay threepence for dying;
And some poor folks cry out 'These are Pharoah like tricks;
To take such unmerciful tale of our bricks';
How great in financing our statesmen have been,
For our ribbons, our shoes, and our hats may be seen;
On this side and that, in the air, on the ground,
By act upon act now so firmly we're bound,
One would think there's not room one new impost to put,
From the crown of the head to the sole of the foot.
Like Job, this John Bull his condition deplores
Very patient indeed, and all cover'd with sores.

ANONYMOUS (*c.* 1795)

CHANGE AND REVOLUTION

THE RISING MIDDLE CLASS

I pray thee tell me what has wit to do with any plodding cit!
Of wit we know not what is meant unless 'tis found in *Cent per
Cent*.
Learning a drug has always been; no Warehouseman will take
it in;

Should practis'd Mercers quit their satin
To look at Greek and long for Latin?
Should the pert upstart Merchant's boy
Look at the Tower and think of Troy?

Or should a Democratic Hatter 'bout old Republics make a clatter?
Should City praters leave their tools to talk by Ciceronian rules
And at our meetings in Guildhall puzzle the mob with Classic brawl?

No, to such things they've no pretence;
No—let them stick to common sense:
You may your ancient bards rehearse,
But there's no common sense in verse;
Not all the classics at your tail
Would weigh an ounce in Reason's scale.
I treat the name of Rome with scorn;
Give me the Commerce of Leghorn.

From Italy's prolific shore the wondrous science was brought o'er,
The bright invention which conveyed such vast facilities to trade:
The DOUBLE ENTRY far outvies All pictur'd sculptured fantasies;
And sure I am, his honour'd name deserves a brighter wreath of Fame,

To whose keen mind the scheme occurr'd,
Than e'er was won by conqueror's sword.
What did the Greeks, pray, know of Trade?
Ulysses, as I've heard it said,

Was full *ten months* oblig'd to roam, before he brought his cargo home:
A voyage in that self-same sea our coasting brigs would make in *three*.

WILLIAM COMBE, *Dr Syntax in Search of the Picturesque* (1809)

THE DECAY OF SUBORDINATION

Johnson. "No man now has the same authority which his father had—except a gaoler. No master has it over his servants: it is diminished in our colleges; nay, in our grammer schools."

Boswell. "What is the cause of this, Sir?"

Johnson. "Why, the coming in of the Scotch" (laughing sarcastically).

Boswell. "That is to say, things have been turned topsy-turvey—But your serious cause."

Johnson. "Why, Sir, there are many causes, the chief of which is, I think, the great increase of money. No man now depends upon the Lord of the Manor, when he can send to another country and fetch provisions. The shoe-black at the entry of my court does not depend on me. I can deprive him but of a penny a day, which he hopes somebody else will bring him; and that penny I must carry to another shoe-black, so the trade suffers nothing. I have explained in my Journey to the Hebrides, how gold and silver destroy feudal subordination. But besides, there is a general relaxation of reverence. No son now depends upon his father as in former times. Paternity used to be considered as of itself a great thing, which had a right to many claims. That is, in general, reduced to very small bounds. My hope is that as anarchy produces tyranny, this extreme relaxation will produce *freni strictio*."

JAMES BOSWELL, *Life of Johnson* (1791)

But the age of chivalry is gone. That of sophisters, economists, and calculators has succeeded; and the glory of Europe is extinguished for ever. Never, never more shall we behold that generous loyalty to rank and sex, that proud submission, that dignified obedience, that subordination of the heart, which kept alive, even in servitude itself, the spirit of an exalted freedom. The unbought grace of life, the cheap defence of nations, the nurse of manly sentiment and heroic enterprise is gone!

EDMUND BURKE, *Reflections on the Revolution in France* (1790)

THE FRENCH REVOLUTION

Oh! pleasant exercise of hope and joy!
For mighty were the auxiliars which then stood
Upon our side, we who were strong in love!
Bliss was it that dawn to be alive,
But to be young was very heaven!—Oh! times,
In which the meagre, stale, forbidding ways
Of custom, law, and statute, took at once
The attraction of a country in romance!
When Reason seemed the most to assert her rights,
When most intent on making of herself
A prime Enchantress—to assist the work
Which then was going forward in her name!
Not favoured spots alone, but the whole earth,
The beauty wore of promise, that which sets
(As at some moment might not be unfelt
Among the bowers of Paradise itself)
The budding rose above the rose full blown.
What temper at the prospect did not wake
To happiness unthought of? The inert
Were roused, and lively natures rapt away!
They who had fed their childhood upon dreams,
The playfellows of fancy, who had made
All powers of swiftness, subtilty, and strength
Their ministers—who in lordly wise had stirred
Among the grandest objects of the sense,
And dealt with whatsoever they found there
As if they had within some lurking right
To wield it—they, too, who, of gentle mood,
Had watched all gentle motions, and to these
Had fitted their own thoughts, schemers more mild,

And in the region of their peaceful selves—
Now was it that both found, the Meek and Lofty
Did both find, helpers to their heart's desire,
And stuff at hand, plastic as they could wish;
Were called upon to exercise their skill,
Not in Utopia, subterranean Fields,
Or some secreted Island, Heaven knows where!
But in the very world, which is the world
Of all of us—the place where in the end
We find our happiness, or not at all!

WILLIAM WORDSWORTH, *The Prelude* (1798–1805)

MODES OF GOVERNMENT

THE FUNCTION OF THE GOVERNMENT

Factions are formed upon opinions; which factions become in effect bodies corporate in the state—nay, factions generate opinions in order to become a centre of union, and to furnish watchwords to parties; and this may make it expedient for government to forbid things in themselves innocent and neutral. I am not fond of defining with precision what the ultimate rights of the sovereign supreme power in providing for the safety of the commonwealth may be, or may not extend to. It will signify very little what my notions, or what their own notions, on the subject may be; because according to the exigence they will take, in fact, the steps which seem to them necessary for the preservation of the whole; for as self-preservation in individuals is the first law of nature, the same will prevail in societies, who will, right or wrong, make that an object paramount to all other rights whatsoever . . .

EDMUND BURKE, *Speech on the Petition of the Unitarians* (1792)

No question has arisen within the records of history that pressed with the importance of the present. It is not whether this or that party shall be in or not, or Whig or Tory, or high or low shall prevail; but whether man shall inherit his rights, and universal civilization take place? Whether the fruits of his labours shall be enjoyed by himself or consumed by the profligacy of Governments?

When, in countries that are called civilized, we see age going to the workhouse and youth going to the gallows, something must be wrong in the system of Government. It would seem, by the exterior appearances of such countries, that all was happiness; but there lies hidden from the eye of common observation, a mass of wretchedness that has scarcely any other chance, than to expire in poverty or infamy. Its entrance into life is marked with the presage of its fate; and until this is remedied, it is in vain to punish.

Civil Government does not consist in executions; but in making that provision for the instruction of youth and the support of age, as to exclude as much as possible profligacy from the one and despair from the other.

THOMAS PAINE, *The Rights of Man* (1791)

REFORM OF THE GOVERNMENT

As for the possibility of the House of Lords preventing ere long a reform of Parliament, I hold it to be the most absurd notion that ever entered into human imagination. I do not mean to be disrespectful, but the attempt of the Lords to stop the progress of reform reminds me very forcibly of the great storm of Sidmouth, and of the conduct of the excellent Mrs Partington on that occasion. In the winter of 1824 there set in a great flood upon the town—the tide rose to an incredible height—the waves rushed in upon the houses, and everything was threatened with destruction! In the midst of this sublime and terrible storm, Dame Partington, who lived upon the beach, was seen at the door of her house, with mop and pattens, trundling her mop, squeezing out the sea-water, and vigorously pushing away the Atlantic Ocean. The Atlantic was roused.

Mrs Partington's spirit was up; but I need not tell you that the contest was unequal. The Atlantic Ocean beat Mrs Partington. She was excellent at a slop, or a puddle, but she should not have meddled with a tempest. Gentlemen, be at your ease—be quiet and steady. You will beat Mrs Partington.

SYDNEY SMITH, *Speech delivered at Taunton* (1831)

PRINCIPLES OF MORALITY

BENEVOLENCE AND UTILITY

Self-love is a principle in human nature of such extensive energy, and the interest of each individual is in general so closely connected with that of the community, that those philosophers were excusable, who fancied that all our concern for the public might be resolved into a concern for our own happiness and preservation. They saw every moment, instances of approbation or blame, satisfaction, or displeasure towards characters and actions; they denominated the objects of these sentiments, *virtues* or *vices*; they observed, that the former had a tendency to increase the happiness, and the latter the misery of mankind; they asked, whether it were possible that we could have any general concern for society, or any disinterested resentment of the injury or welfare of others; they found it simpler to consider all these sentiments as modifications of self-love; and they discovered a pretence at least for this unity of principle, in that close union of interest which is so observable between the public and each individual. But notwithstanding this frequent confusion of interests, it is easy to attain what natural philosophers, after Lord Bacon, have affected to call the *experimentum crucis*, or that experiment which points out the right way in any doubt or ambiguity. We have found instances, in which private interest was separate from public; in which it was even contrary: And yet we observed the moral sentiment to continue, notwithstanding this disjunction of interests. And wherever these distinct interests sensibly concurred, we always found a sensible increase of the sentiment, and a more warm affection to virtue, and detestation of vice, or what we properly call, *gratitude* and *revenge*. Compelled by these instances, we must renounce the theory which accounts for every moral sentiment by the principle of self-love. We must adopt a more public affection, and allow, that the interests of society are not, even on their own account, entirely indifferent to us. Usefulness is only a tendency to a certain end; and it is a contradiction in terms that anything pleases us as means to an end, where the end itself no wise affects us. If usefulness, therefore, be a source of moral sentiment, and if this usefulness be not always considered with a reference to self; it follows that everything which contributes to the happiness of society, recommends itself directly to our approbation and good-will. Here is a principle, which accounts in good part for the origin of morality: and what need we seek for abstruse and remote systems, when there occurs one so obvious and natural?

DAVID HUME, *Enquiry into the Principles of Morals,*
Section V, Part II (1777, second edition)

The merit of benevolence, arising from its utility, and its tendency to promote the good of mankind, has already been explained, and is, no doubt, the source of a *considerable* part of that esteem which is so universally paid to it. But it will also be allowed that the very softness and tenderness of the sentiment, its engaging endearments, its fond expressions, its delicate attentions, and all that flow of mutual confidence and regard which enters into a warm attachment of love and friendship: it will be allowed, I say, that these feelings, being delightful in themselves, are necessarily communicated to the spectators and melt them into the same fondness and delicacy. . . .

As a certain proof that the whole merit of benevolence is not derived from its usefulness, we may observe, that in a kind way of blame, we say, a person is *too good*; when he exceeds his part in society and carries his attentions for others beyond the proper bounds. In like manner we say a man is *too high-spirited, too intrepid, too indifferent about fortune*: reproaches which really, at bottom, imply more esteem than many panegyrics. Being accustomed to rate the merit and demerit of characters by their useful or pernicious tendencies, we cannot forbear applying the epithet of blame, when we discover a sentiment which rises to a degree which is hurtful; but it may happen . . . rather to increase our friendship and concern for the person.

DAVID HUME, *Enquiry into the Principles of Morals*,
Section VII, Part II (1777, second edition)

UNIVERSAL BENEVOLENCE

Since however, the divine goodness is general, and impartial; and he must, consequently, prefer the happiness of the *whole*, to that of any *individuals*, it cannot be his pleasure, that we should consult our own interest, at the expense of that of others. Considering ourselves, therefore, not as separate individuals, but as members of society, another object that we ought to have in view is the welfare of our fellow creatures, and of mankind at large. But still there is no real disagreement among these different rules of conduct, because we are so made, as social beings, that every man provides the most effectually for his own happiness, when he cultivates those sentiments, and pursues that conduct, which, at the same time, most eminently conduce to the welfare of those with whom he is connected. Such is the wisdom of this admirable constitution, that every individual of the system gains his own ends, and those of his maker, by the same means.

JOSEPH PRIESTLEY, *Institutes of Natural and Revealed Religion*,
Vol. I, Part I, Chapter II, Section II, 3 (1782)

E

REASON AND THE SENSES

To make the gratification of our bodily senses the chief end of living would tend to defeat itself; for a man who should have no other end in view would be apt so to overcharge and surfeit his senses that they would become indisposed for their proper functions, and indulgence would occasion nothing but a painful loathing. By intemperance also in eating and drinking, and in all other corporeal pleasures, the powers of the body itself are weakened, and a foundation is laid for disorders the most loathsome to behold, the most painful to endure, and the most fatal in their tendencies and issues. The ingenuity of man cannot contrive any torture so exquisite, and at the same time of so long continuance as those which are occasioned by the irregular indulgence of the senses; whereas temperance and occasional abstinence, is a means of keeping all the bodily organs and senses in their proper tone, disposed to relish their proper gratifications; so that they shall give a man the most true and exquisite enjoyment even of sensual pleasure.

An addictedness to sensual pleasure blunts the faculties of the mind, being injurious to mental apprehension, and all the finer feelings of the soul, and consequently deprives a man of many sources of pleasures which he might otherwise enjoy, and particularly of that most valuable complacency which he might have in his own dispositions and conduct, from a proper and temperate use of the good things of life.

JOSEPH PRIESTLEY, *Institutes of Natural and Revealed Religion*, Vol. I, Part I, Chapter II, Section III, 1 (1782)

It is generally through want of timely *reflection*, that men abandon themselves to irregular indulgences and contract bad habits; so that if they would give themselves time to *think*, and consider deliberately of the nature and consequences of their conduct, they would choose a wise and virtuous course. . . . Were any man therefore truly sensible, that there is no kind of vice to which he does not sacrifice either the health of his body, his reputation with the thinking part of mankind, or even his worldly interest, sometimes all these together, and always the peace and tranquillity of his mind, who would choose to persist in it; admitting that a regard to the good of others, and to the known will of God should have no weight among them; though there are few persons, I believe, who are not more or less influenced even by these generous and disinterested considerations.

JOSEPH PRIESTLEY, *Institutes of Natural and Revealed Religion*,
Vol. I, Part I, Chapter II, Section IV, 1 (1782)

NATURE

Wisdom and Spirit of the universe.
Thou Soul, that art the Eternity of thought!
And giv'st to forms and images a breath
And everlasting motion! not in vain,
By day or star-light, thus from my first dawn
Of childhood didst thou intertwine for me
The passions that build up our human soul;
Not with the mean and vulgar works of Man;
But with high objects, with enduring things,
With life and nature; purifying thus
The elements of feeling and of thought,
And sanctifying by such discipline
Both pain and fear—until we recognize
A grandeur in the beatings of the heart.

WILLIAM WORDSWORTH, *The Influence of Natural Objects* (1798)

UTILITY

Mr Bentham, in private life, is an amiable and exemplary character. He is a little romantic or so, and has dissipated part of a handsome fortune on impractical speculations. He lends an ear to plausible projectors, and, if he cannot prove them wrong in their premises or their conclusions, thinks himself bound *in reason* to stake his money on the venture. Strict logicians are licensed visionaries. . . . Mr Bentham relieves his mind sometimes, after the fatigue of study, by playing on a fine old organ, and has a relish for Hogarth's prints. He turns wooden utensils in a lathe for exercise, and fancies he can turn men in the same manner. He has no great fondness for poetry, and can hardly extract a moral out of Shakespeare. His house is warmed and lighted by steam. He is one of those who prefer the artificial to the natural in most things, and think the mind of man omnipotent. He has a great contempt for out-of-door prospects, for green fields and trees, and is for referring everything to Utility.

WILLIAM HAZLITT, *The Spirit of the Age* (1825)

PRINCIPLES OF SOCIETY

THE NATURE OF LIBERTY

In order to obtain a more distinct and accurate view of the nature of Liberty as such, it will be useful to consider it under the four following general divisions.

First, *physical* liberty; secondly, *moral* liberty; thirdly, *religious* liberty; and fourthly, *civil* liberty; these heads comprise under them all the different kinds of Liberty. And I have placed *civil* liberty last, because I mean to apply to it all I shall say of the other kinds of liberty.

By *Physical* Liberty I mean that principle of spontaneity or self-determination which constitutes us agents; or which gives us a command over our actions rendering them properly *ours*, and not the effects of the operation of any foreign cause. *Moral* Liberty is the power of following, in all circumstances, our sense of right and wrong; or of acting in conformity to our reflecting and moral principles, without being controlled by any contrary principles—*Religious* Liberty signifies the power of exercising without molestation that mode of religion which we think best; or of making the decisions of our own consciences, respecting religious truth, the rule of our conduct, and not of the decision of others.—In like manner; *Civil* liberty is the power of a civil society or state to govern itself by its own discretion; or by laws of its own making, without being subject to any foreign discretion, or to the impositions of any extraneous will or power.

It should be observed that, according to these definitions of the different kinds of liberty, there is one general idea, that runs through them all; I mean, the idea of *self-direction* or *self-government*. Did our volitions originate not with *ourselves* but with some cause over which we have no power; or were we under a necessity of always following some will different from our own, we should want *physical* liberty.

In like manner, he whose perceptions of moral obligation are controlled by his passions has lost *moral* liberty; and the most common language applied to him is, that he wants *self-government*.

He, likewise, who in religion cannot govern himself by his convictions of religious duty, but is obliged to receive formularies of faith and to practice modes of worship imposed on him by others, wants *religious* liberty.—And the community also that is governed, not by itself but by some will independent of it, and over which it has no control wants *civil* liberty.

In all these cases there is a force which stands opposed to the agent's own will; and which, as far as it operates, produces *Servitude*.—In the first case, this force is incompatible with the very idea of voluntary motion; and the subject of it is a mere passive instrument which never *acts*, but is always *acted upon*— In the second case; it is *human authority* in religion requiring conformity to particular modes of faith and worship, and superseding *private judgment*. And in the last case, it is any will distinct from that of the majority of a community, which claims a power of making laws for it and disposing of its property.

This it is, I think, that marks the limit, or that lays the line between *Liberty* and *Slavery*. As far as, in any instance, the operation of any cause comes in to restrain the power of Self-government, so far Slavery is introduced: nor do I think that a preciser idea than this of Liberty and Slavery can be formed.

RICHARD PRICE, On Civil Liberty (1775)

NATURE AND SOCIETY

One difficulty there is that still sticks by us. It has been started indeed but not solved. This is to find a note of distinction—a characteristic mark, whereby to distinguish a society in which there *is* a habit of obedience, and that degree of perfection which is necessary to constitute a state of government, from a society in which there is *not*: a mark, I mean, which shall have a visible determinate commencement; insomuch that the instant of its first appearance shall be distinguishable from the last at which it had not yet appeared. It is only by the help of such a mark that we can be in a condition to determine, at any given time, whether any given society is in a state of government, or in a state of nature, I can find no such mark, I must confess, anywhere, unless it be this: the establishment of names of office: the appearance of a certain man, or set of men, with a certain name, serving to mark them out as objects of obedience: such as King, Sachem, Cacique, Senator, Burgomaster, and the like. This, I think, may serve tolerably well to distinguish a set of men in a state of political union among *themselves* from the *same* set of men not yet in such a state.

JEREMY BENTHAM, A Fragment on Government (1776)

Hitherto we have spoken only (and that but in part) of the natural rights of man. We have now to consider the civil rights of man, and to show how the one originates from the other. Man did not enter into society to become *worse* than he was before, not to have fewer rights than he had before, but to have those rights better secured. His natural rights are the foundation of all his civil rights. But in order to pursue this distinction with more precision, it will be necessary to mark the different qualities of natural and civil rights.

A few words will explain this. Natural rights are those which appertain to man in right of his existence. Of this kind are all the intellectual rights, or rights of the mind, and also all those rights of acting as an individual for his own comfort and happiness, which are not injurious to the natural rights of others. Civil rights are those which appertain to man in right of his being a member of society. Every civil right has for its foundation some natural right pre-existing in the individual, but to the enjoyment of which his individual power is not, in all cases, sufficiently competent. Of this kind are all those which relate to security and protection.

From this short view it will be easy to distinguish between that class of natural rights which man retains after entering into society and those which he throws into the common stock as a member of society.

The natural rights which he retains are all those in which the *power* to execute it is as perfect in the individual as the right itself. Among this class, as is before mentioned, are all the intellectual rights, or rights of the mind; consequently religion is one of those rights. The natural rights which are not retained are all those in which, though the right is perfect in the individual, the power to execute them is defective. They answer not his purpose. A man by natural right has a right to judge in his own cause; and so far as the right of the mind is concerned he never surrenders it. But what availeth it him to judge, if he has not the power to redress? He, therefore, deposits this right in the common stock of society, of which he is a part, and takes the arm of society in preference and in addition to his own. Society *grants* him nothing. Every man is a proprietor in society, and draws on the capital as a matter of right.

THOMAS PAINE, *The Rights of Man*, Part I (1791)

SOCIETY AND CIVILIZATION

Great part of that order which reigns among mankind is not the effect of Government. It has its origin in the principles of society and the natural constitution of man. It existed prior to Government, and would exist if the formality of Government was abolished. The mutual dependence and reciprocal interest which man has upon man, and all the parts of a civilized community upon each other, create that great chain of connection which holds it together. The land-holder, the farmer, the manufacturer, the merchant, the tradesman, and every occupation, prospers by the aid which each receives from the other and from the whole. Common interest regulates their concerns and forms their law; and the laws which common usage ordains have a greater influence than the laws of Government. In fine, society performs for itself almost everything which is ascribed to Government.

To understand the nature and quantity of Government proper for man, it is necessary to attend to his character. As nature created him for social life, she fitted him for the station she intended. In all cases she made his natural wants greater than his individual powers. No one man is capable, without the aid of society, of supplying his own wants; and those wants, acting upon every individual, impel the whole of them into society, as naturally as gravitation acts to a centre.

But she has gone further. She has not only forced man into society by a diversity of wants which the reciprocal aid of each other can supply, but she has implanted in him a system of social affections, which, though not necessary to his existence, are essential to his happiness. There is no period in life when this love for society ceases to act. It begins and ends with our being.

If we examine with attention the composition and constitution of man, the diversity of his wants and talents in different men for reciprocally accommodating the wants of each other, his propensity to society, and, consequently, to preserve the advantages resulting from it, we shall easily discover that a great part of what is called Government is mere imposition.

Government is no farther necessary than to supply the few cases to which society and civilization are not conveniently competent; and instances are not wanting to show, that everything that Government can usefully add thereto, has been performed by the common consent of society, without Government.

For upwards of two years from the commencement of the American War, and to a longer period in several of the American States, there were no established forms of Government. The old Governments had been abolished, and the country was too much occupied in defence to employ its attention in establishing new Governments; yet during this interval order and harmony were preserved as inviolate as in any country in Europe. There is a natural aptness in man, and more so in society, because it embraces a greater variety of abilities and resources, to accommodate itself to whatever situation it is in. The instant formal Government is abolished society begins to act; a general association takes place, and common interest produces common security.

THOMAS PAINE, *The Rights of Man*, Part II, Chapter I (1791)

POPULATION

The ultimate check to population appears then to be a want of food arising necessarily from the different ratios according to which population and food increase. But this ultimate check is never the immediate check, except in cases of actual famine.

The immediate check may be stated to consist in all those customs and all those diseases, which seem to be generated by a scarcity of the means of subsistence; and all those causes, independent of this scarcity, whether of a moral or physical nature, which tend prematurely to weaken and destroy the human frame.

These checks to population, which are constantly operating with more or less force in every society, and keep down the number to the level of the means of subsistence, may be classed under two general heads—the preventive, and the positive checks.

The preventive check, as far as it is voluntary, is peculiar to man, and arises from that distinctive superiority in his reasoning faculties, which enables him to calculate distant consequences. The checks to the indefinite increase of plants and irrational animals are all either positive, or, if preventive, involuntary. But man cannot look around him, and see the distress which frequently presses upon those who have large families; he cannot contemplate his present possessions or earnings, which he now nearly consumes himself, and calculate the amount of each share, when with very little addition they must be divided, perhaps, among seven or eight, without feeling a doubt whether, if he follow the bent of his inclinations, he may be able to support the offspring which he will probably bring into the world. In a state of equality, if such can exist, this would be the simple question. In the present state of society other questions occur. Will he not lower his rank in life, and be obliged to give up in great measure his former habits? Does any mode of employment present itself by which he may reasonably hope to maintain a family? Will he not at any rate subject himself to greater difficulties and more severe labour, than in his single state? Will he not be unable to transmit to his children the same advantages of education and improvement that he had himself possessed? Does he even feel secure that, should he have a large family, his utmost exertions can save them from rags and squalid poverty, and their consequent degradation in the community? And may he not be reduced to the grating necessity of forfeiting his independence, and of being obliged to the sparing hand of charity for support?

T. R. MALTHUS, *Essay on Population* (1798)

II. FROM "AN ENQUIRY CONCERNING POLITICAL JUSTICE"

*Summary of Principles established and reasoned upon
in the Following Work*

THE reader who would form a just estimate of the reasonings of these volumes, cannot perhaps proceed more judiciously, than by examining for himself the truth of these principles, and the support they afford to the various inferences interspersed through the work.

I

The true object of moral and political disquisition, is pleasure or happiness.

The primary, or earliest, class of human pleasures, is the pleasures of the external senses.

In addition to these, man is susceptible of certain secondary pleasures, as the pleasures of intellectual feeling, the pleasures of sympathy, and the pleasures of self-approbation.

The secondary pleasures are probably more exquisite than the primary.

Or, at least,

The most desirable state of man, is that, in which he has access to all these sources of pleasure, and is in possession of a happiness the most varied and uninterrupted.

This state is a state of high civilization.

II

The most desirable condition of the human species, is a state of society.

The injustice and violence of men in a state of society, produced the demand for government.

Government, as it was forced upon mankind by their vices, so has it commonly been the creature of their ignorance and mistake.

Government was intended to suppress injustice, but it offers new occasions and temptations for the commission of it.

By concentrating the force of the community, it gives occasion to wild projects of calamity, to oppression, despotism, war, and conquest.

By perpetuating and aggravating the inequality of property, it fosters many injurious passions, and excites men to the practice of robbery and fraud.

Government was intended to suppress injustice, but its effect has been to embody and perpetuate it.

III

The immediate object of government, is security.

The means employed by government, is restriction, an abridgment of individual independence.

The pleasures of self approbation, together with the right cultivation of all our pleasures, require individual independence.

Without independence man cannot become either wise, or useful, or happy.

Consequently, the most desirable state of mankind, is that which maintains general security, with the smallest encroachment upon individual independence.

IV

The true standard of the conduct of one man towards another, is justice.

Justice is a principle which proposes to itself the production of the greatest sum of pleasure or happiness.

Justice requires that I should put myself in the place of an impartial spectator of human concerns, and divest myself of retrospect to my own predilections.

Justice is a rule of the utmost universality, and prescribes a specific mode of proceeding, in all affairs by which the happiness of a human being may be affected.

V

Duty is that mode of action, which constitutes the best application of the capacity of the individual, to the general advantage.

Right is the claim of the individual, to his share of the benefit arising from his neighbours' discharge of their several duties.

The claim of the individual, is either to the exertion or the forbearance of his neighbours.

The exertions of men in society should ordinarily be trusted to their discretion; their forbearance, in certain cases, is a point of more pressing necessity, and is the direct province of political superintendence, or government.

VI

The voluntary actions of men are under the direction of their feelings.

Reason is not an independent principle, and has no tendency to excite us to action; in a practical view, it is merely a comparison and balancing of different feelings.

Reason, though it cannot excite us to action, is calculated to regulate our conduct, according to the comparative worth it ascribes to different excitements.

It is to the improvement of reason therefore, that we are to look for the improvement of our social condition.

VII

Reason depends for its clearness and strength upon the cultivation of knowledge.

The extent of our progress in the cultivation of knowledge, is unlimited.

Hence it follows:

1. That human inventions, and the modes of social existence, are susceptible of perpetual improvement.
2. That institutions calculated to give perpetuity to any particular mode of thinking, or condition of existence, are pernicious.

VIII

The pleasures of intellectual feeling, and the pleasures of self-approbation, together with the right cultivation of all our pleasures, are connected with soundness of understanding.

Soundness of understanding is inconsistent with prejudice: consequently, as few falsehoods as possible, either speculative or practical, should be fostered among mankind.

Soundness of understanding is connected with freedom of enquiry: consequently, opinion should, as far as public security will admit, be exempted from restraint.

Soundness of understanding is connected with simplicity of manners, and leisure for intellectual cultivation: consequently, a distribution of property extremely unequal, is adverse to the most desirable state of man.

BOOK I

Of the Powers of Man considered in his Social Capacity

CHAPTER I

INTRODUCTION

MANY of the best patriots and most popular writers on the subject of government, appear to have proceeded upon the principles here delineated. They have treated morality and personal happiness as one science, and politics as a different one. But, while they have considered the virtues and pleasures of mankind as essentially independent of civil policy, they have justly remarked, that the security with which the one can be exercised and the other enjoyed, will be decided by the wisdom of our public institutions and the equity with which they are administered; and have earnestly pressed it upon the attention of mankind, not to forget, in the rectitude or happiness of the present moment, those precautions and that 'generous plan of power,' which may tend to render it impregnable to the stratagems of corruption or the insolence of tyranny.

But, while we confess ourselves indebted to the labours of these writers, and perhaps still more to the intrepid language and behaviour of these patriots, we are incited to enquire whether the topic which engaged their attention, be not of higher and more extensive importance than they suspected. Perhaps government is, not merely in some cases the defender, and in other the treacherous foe of the domestic virtues. Perhaps it insinuates itself into our personal dispositions, and insensibly communicates its own spirit to our private transactions. Were not the inhabitants of ancient Greece and Rome indebted in some degree to their political liberties for their excellence in art, and the illustrious theatre they occupy in the moral history of mankind? Are not the governments of modern Europe accountable for the slowness and inconstancy of its literary efforts, and the unworthy selfishness that characterises its inhabitants? Is it not owing to the governments of the East, that that part of the world can scarcely be said to have made any progress in intellect or science?

When scepticism or a spirit of investigation has led us to start these questions, we shall be apt not to stop at them. A wide field of speculation opens itself before us. If government thus insinuate itself in its effects into our most secret retirements, who shall define the extent of its operation? If it be the author of thus much, who shall specify the points from which its influence is excluded? May it not happen, that the grand moral evils that exist in the world, the calamities by which we are so grievously oppressed, are to be traced to political institution as their source, and that their removal is only to be expected from its correction? May it not be found, that the attempt to alter the morals of mankind singly and in detail is an injudicious and futile undertaking; and that the change of their political institutions must keep pace with their advancement in knowledge, if we expect to secure to them a real and permanent improvement? To prove the affirmative of these questions shall be the business of this first book.

The method to be pursued for that purpose, shall be, first, to take a concise survey of the evils existing in political society; secondly, to show that these evils are to be ascribed to public institutions; and thirdly, that they are not the inseparable condition of our existence, but admit of removal and remedy.

CHAPTER II

HISTORY OF POLITICAL SOCIETY

IT is an old observation, that the history of mankind is little else than a record of crimes. Society comes recommended to us by its tendency to supply our wants and promote our well-being. If we consider the human species, as they were found previously to the existence of political society, it is difficult not to be impressed with emotions of melancholy. But, though the chief purpose of society is to defend us from want and inconvenience, it effects this purpose in a very imperfect degree. We are still liable to casualties, disease, infirmity, and death. Famine destroys its thousands, and pestilence its ten thousands. Anguish visits us under every variety of form, and day after day is spent in languor and dissatisfaction. Exquisite pleasure is a guest of very rare approach, and not less short continuance.

But, though the evils that arise to us from the structure of the material universe are neither trivial nor few, yet the history of political societys sufficiently shows that man is of all other beings the most formidable enemy to man. Among the various schemes that he has formed to destroy and plague his kind, war is the most terrible. . . .

Let us examine Europe, the most civilised and favoured quarter of the world, or even those countries of Europe which are thought the most enlightened.

France was wasted by successive battles during a whole century, for the question of the Salic law, and the claim of the Plantagenets. Scarcely was this contest terminated, before the religious wars broke out, some idea of which we may form from the siege of Rochelle, where, of fifteen thousand persons shut up, eleven thousand perished of hunger and misery; and from the massacre of Saint Bartholomew, in which the numbers assassinated were forty thousand. This quarrel was appeased by Henry the Fourth, and succeeded by the thirty years' war

F

in Germany for superiority with the house of Austria, and afterwards by the military transactions of Louis the Fourteenth.

In England the war of Cressy and Agincourt only gave place to the civil war of York and Lancaster, and again after an interval to the war of Charles the First and his parliament. No sooner was the constitution settled by the revolution, than we were engaged in a wide field of continental hostilities by King William, the Duke of Marlborough, Maria Theresa and the King of Prussia.

And what are in most cases the pretences upon which war is undertaken? What rational man could possibly have given himself the least disturbance, for the sake of choosing whether Henry the Sixth or Edward the Fourth should have the style of King of England? What Englishman could reasonably have drawn his sword for the purpose of rendering his country an inferior dependency of France, as it must necessarily have been if the ambition of the Plantagenets had succeeded? What can be more deplorable, than to see us first engage eight years in war rather than suffer the haughty Maria Theresa to live with a diminished sovereignty or in a private station; and then eight years more to support the free-booter who had taken advantage of her helpless condition?

The usual causes of war are excellently described by Swift.

Sometimes the quarrel between two princes is to decide which of them shall dispossess a third of his dominions, where neither of them pretends to any right. Sometimes one prince quarrels with another, for fear the other should quarrel with him. Sometimes a war is entered upon because the enemy is too strong; and sometimes because he is too weak. Sometimes our neighbours want the things which we have, or have the things which we want; and we both fight, till they take ours, or give us theirs. It is very justifiable cause of war to invade a country after the people have been wasted by famine, destroyed by pestilence, or embroiled by factions among themselves. It is justifiable to enter into a war against our nearest ally, when one of his towns lies convenient for us, or a territory of land that would render our dominions round and compact. If a prince sends forces into a nation where the people are poor and ignorant, he may lawfully put the half of them to death, and make slaves of the rest, in order to civilise and reduce them from their barbarous way of living. It is a very kingly, honourable and frequent practice, when one prince desires the assistance of another to secure him against an invasion, that the assistant, when he has driven out the invader, should seize on the dominions himself, and kill, imprison or banish the prince he came to relieve.

If we turn from the foreign transactions of states with each other, to the principles of their domestic policy, we shall not find much greater reason to be satisfied. A numerous class of mankind are held down in a state of abject penury, and are continually prompted by disappointment and distress to commit violence upon their more fortunate neighbours. The only mode which is employed to repress this violence, and to maintain the order and peace of society, is punishment. Whips, axes, and gibbets, dungeons, chains, and racks are the most approved and established methods of persuading men to obedience, and impressing upon their minds the lessons of reason. There are few subjects upon which human ingenuity has been more fully displayed than in inventing instruments of torture. The lash of the whip a thousand times repeated and flagrant on the back of the defenceless victim, the bastinado on the soles of the feet, the dislocation of limbs, the fracture of bones, the faggot and the stake, the cross, impaling, and the mode of drifting pirates on the Volga, make but a small part of the catalogue. When Damiens, the maniac, was arraigned for his abortive attempt on the life of Louis the Fifteenth of France, a council of anatomists was summoned, to deliberate how a human being might be destroyed with the longest protracted and most diversified agony. Hundreds of victims are annually sacrificed at the shrine of positive law and political institution.

Add to this the species of government which prevails over nine-tenths of the globe, which is despotism: a government, as Locke justly observes, altogether "vile and miserable," and "more to be deprecated than anarchy itself."

Certainly every man who takes a dispassionate survey of this picture, will feel himself inclined to pause respecting the necessity of the havoc which is thus made of his species, and to question whether the established methods for protecting mankind against the caprices of each other are the best that can be devised. He will be at a loss which of the two to pronounce most worthy of regret, the misery that is inflicted, or the depravity by which it is produced. If this be the unalterable allotment of our nature, the eminence of our rational faculties must be considered as rather an abortion than a substantial benefit; and we shall not fail to lament that, while in some respects we are elevated above the brutes, we are in so many important ones destined for ever to remain their inferiors.

CHAPTER III

SPIRIT OF POLITICAL INSTITUTIONS

FIRST then it is to be observed, that, in the most refined states of Europe, the inequality of property has risen to an alarming height. Vast numbers of their inhabitants are deprived of almost every accommodation that can render life tolerable or secure. Their utmost industry scarcely suffices for their support. The women and children lean with an insupportable weight upon the efforts of the man, so that a large family has in the lower orders of life become a proverbial expression for an uncommon degree of poverty and wretchedness. If sickness or some of those casualties which are perpetually incident to an active and laborious life, be added to these burthens, the distress is yet greater.

It seems to be agreed that in England there is less wretched-ness and distress than in most of the kingdoms of the continent. In England the poors' rates amount to the sum of two millions sterling per annum. It has been calculated that one person in seven of the inhabitants of this country derives at some period of his life assistance from this fund. If to this we add the persons, who, from pride, a spirit of independence, or the want of a legal settlement, though in equal distress receive no such assistance, the proportion will be considerably increased.

I lay no stress upon the accuracy of this calculation; the general fact is sufficient to give us an idea of the greatness of the abuse. The consequences that result are placed beyond the reach of contradiction. A perpetual struggle with the evils of poverty, if frequently ineffectual, must necessarily render many of the sufferers desperate. A painful feeling of their oppressed situation will itself deprive them of the power of surmounting it. The superiority of the rich, being thus unmercifully exercised, must inevitably expose them to reprisals; and the poor man will be induced to regard the state of society as a state of war, an unjust combination, not for protecting every man in his rights and securing to him the means of existence, but for engrossing all its advantages to a few favoured indi-viduals, and reserving for the portion of the Rest want, dependence and misery.

A second source of those destructive passions by which the peace of society is interrupted, is to be found in the luxury, the pageantry and magnificence, with which enormous wealth is usually accompanied. Human beings are capable of encoun-tering with cheerfulness considerable hardships, when those hardships are impartially shared with the rest of the society, and they are not insulted with the spectacle of indolence and ease in others, no way deserving of greater advantages than themselves. But it is a bitter aggravation of their own calamity, to have the privileges of others forced on their observation, and, while they are perpetually and vainly endeavouring to secure for themselves and their families the poorest conveniences, to find others revelling in the fruits of their labours. This aggravation is assiduously administered to them under most of the political establishments at present in existence. There is a numerous class of individuals, who, though rich, have neither brilliant talents nor sublime virtues; and, however highly they may prize their education, their affability, their superior polish and the elegance of their manners, have a secret consciousness that they possess nothing by which they can so securely assert their pre-eminence and keep their inferiors at a distance, as the splendour of their equipage, the magnificence of their retinue, and the sumptuousness of their entertainments. The poor man is struck with this exhibition; he feels his own miseries; he knows how unwearied are his efforts to obtain a slender pittance of this prodigal waste; and he mistakes opulence for felicity. He cannot persuade himself that an embroidered garment may frequently cover an aching heart.

A third disadvantage that is apt to connect poverty with discontent, consists in the insolence and usurpation of the rich. If the poor man would in other respects compose himself in philosophic indifference, and, conscious that he possesses everything that is truly honourable to man as his rich neighbour, would look upon the rest as beneath his envy, his neighbour will not permit him to do so. He seems as if he could never be satisfied with his possessions, unless he can make the spectacle of them grating to others; and that honest self-esteem, by which his inferior might otherwise attain to tranquility, is rendered the instrument of galling him with oppression and injustice. In many countries justice is avowedly a subject of solicitation, and the man of the highest rank and most splendid connections almost infallibly carries his cause against the unprotected and friendless. In countries where this shameless practice is not established, justice is frequently a matter of expensive purchase, and the man with the longest purse is proverbially victorious. A consciousness of these facts must be expected to render the rich little cautious of offence in his dealings with the poor, and to inspire him with a temper overbearing, dictatorial and tyrannical. Nor does this indirect oppression satisfy his despotism. The rich are in all such countries directly or indirectly the legislators of the state; and of consequence are perpetually reducing oppression into a system, and depriving the poor of that little commonage of nature, which might otherwise still have remained to them. . . .

Such are the causes, that, in different degrees under the different governments of the world, prompt mankind openly or secretly to encroach upon the property of each other. Let us consider how far they admit either of remedy or aggravation from political institution. Whatever tends to decrease the injuries attendant upon poverty, decreases at the same time the inordinate desire and the enormous accumulation of wealth. Wealth is not pursued for its own sake, and seldom for the sensual gratifications it can purchase, but for the same reasons that ordinarily prompt men to the acquisition of learning, eloquence and skill, for the love of distinction and the fear of contempt. How few would prize the possession of riches, if they were condemned to enjoy their equipage, their palaces and their entertainments in solitude, with no eye to wonder at their magnificence, and no sordid observer ready to convert that wonder into an adulation of the owner? If admiration were not generally deemed the exclusive property of the rich, and contempt the constant lacquey of poverty, the love of gain would cease to be an universal passion. Let us consider in what respects political institution is rendered subservient to this passion.

First then, legislation is in almost every country grossly the favourer of the rich against the poor. Such is the character of the game-laws, by which the industrious rustic is forbidden to destroy the animal that preys upon the hopes of his future subsistence, or to supply himself with the food that unsought thrusts itself in his path. Such was the spirit of the late revenue-laws of France, which in several of their provisions fell exclusively upon the humble and industrious, and exempted from their operation those who were best able to support it. Thus in England the land-tax at this moment produces half a million less than it did a century ago, while the taxes on consumption have experienced an addition of thirteen millions per annum during the same period. This is an attempt, whether effectual or no, to throw the burthen from the rich upon the poor, and as such is an example of the spirit of legislation. Upon the same principle robbery and other offences, which the wealthier part of the community have no temptation to commit, are treated as capital crimes, and attended with the most rigorous, often the most inhuman punishments. The rich are encouraged to associate for the execution of the most partial and oppressive positive laws; monoploies and patents are lavishly dispensed to such as are able to purchase them; while the most vigilant policy is employed to prevent combinations of the poor to fix the price of labour, and they are deprived of the benefit of that prudence and judgment which would select the scene of their industry.

Secondly, the administration of law is not less iniquitous than the spirit in which it is framed. Under the late government of France the office of judge was a matter of purchase, partly by an open price advanced to the crown, and partly by a secret douceur paid to the minister. He, who knew best how to manage his market in the retail trade of justice, could afford to purchase the good will of its functions at the highest price. To the client justice was avowedly made an object of personal solicitation; and a powerful friend, a handsome woman, or a proper present, were articles of much greater value, than a good cause. In England the criminal law is administered with greater impartiality so far as regards the trial itself; but the number of capital offences, and of consequence the frequency of pardons, open a wide door to favour and abuse. In causes relating to property the practice of law is arrived at such a pitch as to render its nominal impartiality utterly nugatory. The length of our chancery suits, the multiplied appeals from court to court, the enormous fees of counsel, attornies, secretaries, clerks, the drawing of briefs, bills, replications and rejoinders, and what has sometimes been called the 'glorious uncertainty' of the law, render it frequently more advisable to resign a property than to contest it, and particularly exclude the impoverished claimant from the faintest hope of redress.

Thirdly, the inequality of conditions usually maintained by political institution, is calculated greatly to enhance the imagined excellence of wealth. In the ancient monarchies of the east, and in Turkey at the present day, an eminent station could scarcely fail to excite implicit deference. The timid inhabitant trembled before his superior; and would have thought it little less than blasphemy, to touch the veil drawn by the proud satrap over his inglorious origin. The same principles were extensively prevalent under the feudal system. The vassal, who was regarded as a sort of live stock upon the estate, and knew no appeal from the arbitrary fiat of his lord, would scarcely venture to suspect that he was of the same species. This however constituted an unnatural and violent situation. There is a propensity in man to look further than the outside; and to come with a writ of enquiry into the title of the upstart and the successful. By the operation of these causes the insolence of wealth has been in some degree moderated. Meantime it cannot be pretended that even among ourselves the inequality is not strained, so as to give birth to very unfortunate consequences. If, in the enormous degree in which it prevails in some parts of the world, it wholly debilitate and emasculate the human race, we shall see some reason to believe that, even in the milder state in which we are accustomed to behold it, it is still pregnant with the most mischievous effects.

CHAPTER IV

The Characters of Men originate in their External Circumstances

Thus far we have argued from historical facts, and from them have collected a very strong presumptive evidence, that political institutions have a more powerful and extensive influence, than it has been generally the practice to ascribe to them.

But we can never arrive at precise conceptions relative to this part of the subject, without entering into an analysis of the human mind, and endeavouring to ascertain the nature of the causes by which its operations are directed. Under this branch of the subject I shall attempt to prove two things; first, that the actions and dispositions of mankind are the offspring of circumstances and events, and not of any original determination that they bring into the world; and, secondly, that the great stream of our voluntary actions essentially depends, not upon the direct and immediate impulses of sense, but upon the decisions of the understanding. If these proportions can be sufficiently established, it will follow that the happiness men are able to attain, is proportioned to the justness of the opinions they take as guides in the pursuit; and it will only remain, for the purpose of applying these premises to the point under consideration, that we should demonstrate the opinions of men to be, for the most part, under the absolute control of political institution. . . .

These truths will be brought to our minds with much additional evidence, if we compare in this respect the case of brutes with that of men. Among the inferior animals, breed is a circumstance of considerable importance, and a judicious mixture and preservation in this point is found to be attended with the most unequivocal results. But nothing of that kind appears to take place in our own species. A generous blood, a gallant and fearless spirit is by no means propagated from father to son. When a particular appellation is granted, as is usually practised in the existing governments of Europe, to designate the descendants of a magnanimous ancestry, we do not find, even with all the arts of modern education to assist, that such descendants are the legitimate representatives of departed heroism. Whence comes this difference? Probably from the more irresistible operation of moral causes. It is not impossible that among savages those differences would be conspicuous, which with us are annihilated. It is not unlikely that, if men, like brutes, were withheld from the more considerable means of intellectual improvement, if they derived nothing from the discoveries and sagacity of their ancestors, if each individual had to begin absolutely *de novo* in the discipline and arrangement of his ideas, blood or whatever other circumstances distinguish one man from another at the period of his nativity, would produce as memorable effects in man, as they now do in those classes of animals that are deprived of our advantages. Even in the case of brutes, education and care on the part of man seem to be nearly indispensible, if we would not have the foal of the finest racer degenerate to the level of the cart-horse. In plants the peculiarities of soil decide in a great degree upon the future properties of each. But who would think of forming the character of a human being by the operations of heat and cold, dryness and moisture upon the animal frame? With us moral considerations swallow up the effects of every other accident. Present a pursuit to the mind, convey to it the apprehension of calamity or advantage, excite it by motives of aversion or motives of affection, and the slow and silent influence of material causes perishes like dews at the rising of the sun.

The result of these considerations is, that at the moment of birth man has really a certain character, and each man a character different from his fellows. The accidents which pass during the months of percipiency in the womb of the mother, produce a real effect. Various external accidents, unlimited as to the period of their commencement, modify in different ways the elements of the animal frame. Every thing in the universe is linked and united together. No event, however minute and imperceptible, is barren of a train of consequences, however comparatively evanescent those consequences may in some instances be found. If there have been philosophers that have asserted otherwise, and taught that all minds from the period of birth were precisely alike, they have reflected discredit by such an incautious statement upon the truth they proposed to defend.

But, though the original differences of man and man be arithmetically speaking something, speaking in the way of a general and comprehensive estimate they may be said to be almost nothing. If the early impressions of our childhood may by a skilful observer be as it were obliterated almost as soon as made, how much less can the confused and unpronounced impressions of the womb, be expected to resist the multiplicity of ideas that successively contribute to wear out their traces? If the temper of the man appear in many instances to be totally changed, how can it be supposed that there is any thing permanent and inflexible in the propensities of a new-born infant: and, if not in the character of the disposition, how much less in that of the understanding?

Speak the language of truth and reason to your child, and be under no apprehension for the result. Show him what you recommend is valuable and desirable, and fear not but he will desire it. Convince his understanding, and you enlist all his powers animal and intellectual in your service. How long has the genius of education been disheartened and unnerved by the pretence that man is born all that it is possible for him to become? How long has the jargon imposed upon the world, which would persuade us that in instructing a man you do not add to, but unfold his stores? The miscarriages of education do not proceed from the boundedness of its powers, but from the mistakes with which it is accompanied. We often inspire disgust, where we mean to infuse desire. We are wrapped up in ourselves, and do not observe, as we ought, step by step the sensations that pass in the mind of our hearer. We mistake compulsion for persuasion, and delude ourselves into the belief that despotism is the road to the heart.

Education will proceed with a firm step and with genuine lustre, when those who conduct it shall know what a vast field it embraces; when they shall be aware, that the effect, the question whether the pupil shall be a man of perseverance and enterprise or a stupid and inanimate dolt, depends upon the powers of those under whose direction he is placed, and the skill with which those powers shall be applied. Industry will be exerted with tenfold alacrity, when it shall be generally confessed that there are no obstacles to our improvement, which do not yield to the powers of industry. Multitudes will never exert the energy necessary to extraordinary success, till they shall dismiss the prejudices that fetter them, get rid of the chilling system of occult and inexplicable causes, and consider the human mind as an intelligent agent, guided by motives and prospects presented to the understanding, and not by causes of which we have no proper cognisance and can form no calculation. . . .

It remains to be considered what share political institution and forms of government occupy in the education of every human being. Their degree of influence depends upon two essential circumstances.

First, it is nearly impossible to oppose the education of the preceptor, and the education we derive from the forms of government under which we live, to each other; and therefore, however powerful the former of these may be, absolutely considered, it can never enter the lists with the latter upon equal terms. Should any one talk to us of rescuing a young person from the sinister influence of a corrupt government by the power of education, it will be fair to ask, who is the preceptor by whom this task is to be effected? Is he born in the ordinary mode of generation, or does he descend among us from the skies? Has his character been in no degree modified, by that very influence he undertakes to counteract? It is beyond all controversy, that men who live in a state of equality, or that approached equality, will be frank, ingenuous and intrepid in their carriage; while those who inhabit where a great disparity of ranks has prevailed, will be distinguished by coldness, irresoluteness, timidity and caution. Will the preceptor in question be altogether superior to these qualities? Which of us is there who utters his thoughts, in the fearless and explicit manner that true wisdom would prescribe? Who, that is sufficiently critical and severe, does not detect himself every hour in some act of falsehood or equivocation, that example and early habits have planted too deeply to be eradicated? But the question is not, what extraordinary persons can be found, who may shine illustrious exceptions to the prevailing degeneracy of their neighbours. As long as parents and teachers in general shall fall under the established rule, it is clear that politics and modes of government will educate and infect us all. They poison our minds, before we can resist, or so much as uspect their malignity. Like the barbarous directors of the Eastern seraglios, they deprive us of our virility and fit us for their despicable employment from the cradle. So false is the opinion that has too generally prevailed, that politics is an affair with which ordinary men have little concern.

Secondly, supposing the preceptor had all the qualifications that can reasonably be imputed, let us recollect for a moment what are the influences with which he would have to struggle. Political institution, by the consequences with which it is pregnant, strongly suggests to every one who enters within its sphere, what is the path he should avoid as well as what he should pursue. Under a government fundamentally erroneous, he will see intrepid virtue proscribed, and a servile and corrupt spirit uniformly encouraged. But morality itself is nothing but a calculation of consequences. What strange confusion will the spectacle of that knavery which is universally practised through all the existing classes of society, produce in the mind? The preceptor cannot go out of the world, or prevent the intercourse of his pupil with human beings of a character different from his own. Attempts of this kind are generally unhappy, stamped with the impression of artifice, intolerance and usurpation. From earliest infancy therefore there will be two principles contending for empire, the peculiar and elevated system of the preceptor, and the grovelling views of the great mass of mankind. These will generate confusion, uncertainty and irresolution. At no period of life will the effect correspond to what it would have been, if the community were virtuous and wise. But its effect, obscure and imperceptible for a time, may be expected to burst into explosion at the period of puberty. When the pupil first becomes master of his own actions, and chooses his avocations and his associates, he will necessarily be acquainted with many things of which before he had very slender notions. At this time the follies of the world wear their most alluring face. He can scarcely avoid imagining that he has hitherto laboured under some species of delusion. Delusion, when detected, causes him upon whom it was practised to be indignant and restive. The only chance which remains, is that, after a time, he should be recalled and awakened: and against this chance there are the progressive enticements of society; sensuality, ambition, sordid interest, false ridicule, and the incessant decay of that unblemished purity which attended him in his outset. The best that can be expected, is that he should return at last to sobriety and truth, with a mind debilitated and relaxed by repeated errors, and a moral constitution in which the seeds of degeneracy have been deeply and extensively sown.

CHAPTER V

THE VOLUNTARY ACTIONS OF MEN ORIGINATE IN THEIR OPINIONS

IN the meantime it is obvious to remark, that the perfection of the human character consists in approaching as nearly as possible to the perfectly voluntary state. We ought to be upon all occasions prepared to render a reason of our actions. We should remove ourselves to the furthest distance from the state of mere inanimate machines, acted upon by causes of which they have no understanding. We should be cautious of thinking it a sufficient reason for an action, that we are accustomed to perform it, and that we once thought it right. The human understanding has so powerful a tendency to improvement, that it is more probable that, in many instances, the arguments which once appeared to us sufficient, would upon re-examination appear inadequate and futile. We should therefore subject them to perpetual revisal. In our speculative opinions and our practical principles we should never consider the book of enquiry as shut. We should accustom ourselves not to forget the reasons that produced our determination, but be ready upon all occasions clearly to announce and fully to enumerate them. . . .

When we discourse of the comparative powers of appetite and reason, we speak of those actions, which have the consent of the mind, and partake of the nature of voluntary. The question neither is nor deserves to be, respecting cases where no choice is exerted, and no preference shown. Every man is aware, that the cases, into which volition enters either for a part or the whole, are sufficiently numerous, to decide upon all that is most important in the events of our life. It follows therefore that, in the contention of sense and reason, it cannot be improbable to hope that the opinion which is intrinsically the best founded, shall ultimately prevail.

But let us examine a little minutely these pleasures of sense, the attractions of which are supposed to be so irresistible. In reality they are in no way enabled to maintain their hold upon us, but by means of the adscititious ornaments with which they are assiduously connected. Reduce them to their true nakedness, and they would be generally despised. Where almost is the man, who would sit down with impatient eagerness to the most splendid feast, the most exquisite viands and highly flavoured wines, "taste after taste upheld with kindliest change," if he must sit down alone, and it were not relieved and assisted by the more exalted charms of society, conversation and mutual benevolence? Strip the commerce of the sexes of all its attendant circumstances; and the effect would be similar. Tell a man that all women, so far as sense is concerned, are nearly alike. Bid him therefore take a partner without any attention to the symmetry of her person, her vivacity, the voluptuous softness of her temper, the affectionate kindness of her feelings, her imagination or her wit. You would probably instantly convince him that the commerce itself, which by superficial observers is put for the whole, is the least important branch of the complicated consideration to which it belongs. It is probable that he who should form himself with the greatest care upon a system of solitary sensualism, would come at last to a decision not very different from that which Epicurus is said to have adopted, in favour of fresh herbs and water from the spring. . . .

The corollaries respecting political truth, deducible from the simple proposition, which seems clearly established by the reasonings of the present chapter, that the voluntary actions of men are in all instances conformable to the deductions of their understanding, are of the highest importance. Hence we may infer what are the hopes and prospects of human improvement. The doctrine which may be founded upon these principles, may perhaps best be expressed in the five following propositions. Sound reasoning and truth, when adequately communicated, must always be victorious over error. Sound reasoning and truth are capable of being so communicated. Truth is omnipotent. The vices and moral weakness of man are not invincible. Man is perfectible, or in other words susceptible of perpetual improvement. . . .

The term perfectible, thus explained, not only does not imply the capacity of being brought to perfection, but stands in express opposition to it. If we could arrive at perfection, there would be an end to our improvement. There is however one thing of great importance that it does imply: every perfection or excellence that human beings are competent to conceive, human beings, unless in cases that are palpably unequivocally excluded by the structure of their frame, are competent to attain.

This is an inference which immediately follows from the omnipotence of truth. Every truth that is capable of being communicated, is capable of being brought home to the conviction of the mind. Every principle which can be brought home to the conviction of the mind, will infallibly produce a correspondent effect upon the conduct. If there were not something in the nature of man incompatible with absolute perfection, the doctrine of the omnipotence of truth would afford no small probability that he would one day reach it. Why is the perfection of man impossible?

The idea of absolute perfection is scarcely within the grasp of human understanding. If science were more familiarised to speculations of this sort, we should perhaps discover that the notion itself was pregnant with absurdity and contradiction.

It is not necessary in this argument to dwell upon the limited nature of the human faculties. We can neither be present to all places nor to all times. We cannot penetrate into the essences of things, or rather we have no sound and satisfactory knowledge of things external to ourselves, but merely of our own sensations. We cannot discover the causes of things, or ascertain that in the antecedent which connects it with the consequent, and discern nothing but their contiguity. With what pretence can a being thus shut in on all sides lay claim to absolute perfection?

But not to insist upon these considerations, there is one principle in the human mind, which must for ever exclude us from arriving at a close of our acquisitions, and confine us to perpetual progress. The human mind, so far as we are acquainted with it, is nothing else but a faculty of perception. All our knowledge, all our ideas, every thing we possess as intelligent beings, comes from impression. All the minds that exist, set out from absolute ignorance. They received first one impression, and then a second. As the impressions became more numerous, and were stored by the help of memory, and combined by the faculty of association, so the experience increased, and with the experience the knowledge, the wisdom, every thing that distinguishes man from what we understand by a 'clod of the valley.' This seems to be a simple and incontrovertible history of intellectual being; and, if it be true, then as our accumulations have been incessant in the time that is gone, so, as long as we continue to perceive, to remember or reflect, they must perpetually increase.

CHAPTER VIII

Human Inventions
susceptible of Perpetual Improvement

Before we proceed to the direct subject of the present enquiry, it may not be improper to resume the subject of human improveableness, and consider it in a somewhat greater detail. An opinion has been extensively entertained, "that the differences of the human species in different ages and countries, particularly so far as relates to moral principles of conduct, are extremely insignificant and trifling; that we are deceived in this respect by distances and confounded by glare; but that in reality the virtues and vices of men, collectively taken, always have remained, and of consequence," it is said, "always will remain, nearly at the same point."

The erroneousness of this opinion will perhaps be more completely exposed, by a summary recollection of the actual history of our species, than by the closest deductions of abstract reason. We will in this place simply remind the reader of the great changes which man has undergone as an intellectual being, entitling us to infer the probability of improvements not less essential, to be realised in future. The conclusion to be deduced from this delineation, that his moral improvements will in some degree keep pace with his intellectual, and his actions correspond with his opinions, must depend for its force upon the train of reasoning which has already been brought forward under that head.

Let us carry back our minds to man in his original state, as being capable of impressions and knowledge to an unbounded extent, but not having as yet received the one or cultivated the other; let us contrast this being with all that science and genius have effected; and from hence we may form some idea what it is of which human nature is capable. It is to be remembered, that this being did not, as now, derive assistance from the communications of his fellows, nor had his feeble and crude conceptions amended by the experience of successive centuries; but that in the state we are figuring all men were equally ignorant. The field of improvement was before them, but for every step in advance they were to be indebted to their untutored efforts. Nor is it of consequence whether such was actually the progress of mind, or whether, as others teach, the progress was abridged, and man was immediately advanced half way to the end of his career by the interposition of the author of his nature. In any case it is an allowable, and will be found no unimproving speculation, to consider mind as it is in itself, and to enquire what would have been its history if, immediately upon its production, it had been left to be acted upon by those ordinary laws of the universe with whose operation we are acquainted.

One of the acquisitions most evidently requisite as a preliminary to our present improvements, is that of language. But it is impossible to conceive an acquisition, that must have been in its origin more different from what at present it is found, or that less promised that copiousness and refinement it has since exhibited.

Its beginning was probably from those involuntary cries, which infants, for example, are found to utter in the earliest stages of their existence, and which previously to the idea of exciting pity or procuring assistance, spontaneously arise from the operation of pain upon our animal frame. These cries, when actually uttered, become a subject of perception to him by whom they are uttered; and, being observed to be constantly associated with certain antecedent impressions and to excite the idea of those impressions in the hearer, may afterwards be repeated from reflection and the desire of relief. Eager desire to communicate any information to another, will also prompt us to utter some simple sound for the purpose of exciting attention: this sound will probably frequently recur to organs unpractised to variety, and will at length stand as it were by convention for the information intended to be conveyed. But the distance is extreme from these simple modes of communication, which we possess in common with some of the inferior animals, to all the analysis and abstraction which languages require.

Abstraction indeed, though, as it is commonly understood, it be one of the sublimest operations of mind, is in some sort coeval with and inseparable from the existence of mind. The next step to simple perception is that of comparison, or the coupling together of two ideas and the perception of their resemblances and differences. Without comparison there can be no preference, and without preference no voluntary action: though it must be acknowledged, that this comparison is an operation which may be performed by the mind without adverting to its nature, and that neither the brute nor the savage has a consciousness of the several steps of the intellectual progress. Comparison immediately leads to imperfect abstraction. The sensation of today is classed, if similar, with the sensation of yesterday, and an inference is made respecting the conduct to be adopted. Without this degree of abstraction, the faint dawnings of language already described, could never have existed. Abstraction, which was necessary to the first existence of language, is again assisted in its operations by language. That generalisation, which is implied in the very notion of a thinking being, being thus embodied and rendered a matter of sensible impression, makes the mind acquainted with its own powers, and creates a restless desire after further progress.

But, though it be by no means impossible, to trace the causes that concurred to the production of language, and to prove them adequate to their effect, it does not the less appear that this is an acquisition of slow growth and inestimable value. The very steps, were we to pursue them, would appear like an endless labyrinth. The distance is immeasurable, between the three or four vague and inarticulate sounds uttered by animals, and the copiousness of lexicography or the regularity of grammar. The general and special names by which things are at first complicated and afterwards divided, the names by which properties are separated from their substances, and powers from both, the comprehensive distribution of parts of speech, verbs, adjectives and particles, the inflections of words by which the change of their terminations changes their meaning through a variety of shadings, their concords and their governments, all of them present us with such a boundless catalogue of science, that he, who on the one hand did not know that the task had been actually performed, or who on the other was not intimately acquainted with the progressive nature of mind, would pronounce the accomplishment of them impossible.

BOOK II

Principles of Society

CHAPTER I

INTRODUCTION

THE regulations to which the conduct of men living in society ought to be conformed, may be considered in two ways: first, those moral laws which are enjoined upon us by the dictates of enlightened reason; and, secondly, those principles a deviation from which the interest of the community may be supposed to render it proper to repress by sanctions and punishment.

Morality is that system of conduct which is determined by a consideration of the greatest general good: he is entitled to the highest moral approbation, whose conduct is, in the greatest number of instances, or in the most momentous instances, governed by views of benevolence, and made subservient to public utility. In like manner the only regulations which any political authority can be justly entitled to inforce, are such as are best adapted to public utility. Consequently, just political regulations are nothing more than a certain select part of moral law. The supreme power in a state ought not, in the strictest sense, to require any thing of its members, that an understanding sufficiently enlightened would not prescribe without such interference.

These considerations seem to lead to the detection of a mistake which has been very generally committed, by political writers of our own country. They have for the most part confined their researches to the question of What is a just political authority or the most eligible form of government, consigning to others the delineation of right principles of conduct and equitable regulations. But there appears to be something preposterous in this mode of proceeding. A well constituted government is only the means for enforcing suitable regulations. One form of government is preferable to another in exact proportion to the security it affords, that nothing shall be done in the name of the community, which is not conducive to the welfare of the whole. The question therefore, What it is which is thus conducive, is upon every account entitled to the first place in our disquisitions.

One of the ill-consequences which have resulted from this distorted view of the science of politics, is a notion very generally entertained, that a community, or society of men, has a right to lay down whatever rules it may think proper for its own observance. This will presently be proved to be an erroneous position. It may be prudent in an individual to submit in some cases to the usurpation of a majority; it may be unavoidable in a community to proceed upon the imperfect and erroneous views that they shall chance to entertain: but this is a misfortune entailed upon us by the nature of government, and not a matter of right.

A second ill-consequence that has arisen from this proceeding, is that, politics having been thus violently separated from morality, government itself has no longer been compared with its true criterion. Instead of enquiring what species of government was most conducive to the public welfare, an unprofitable disquisition has been instituted respecting the probable origin of government; and its different forms have been estimated, not by the consequences with which they were pregnant, but the source from which they sprung. Hence men have been prompted to look back to the folly of their ancestors, rather than forward to the benefits derivable from the improvements of human knowledge. Hence, in investigating their rights, they have recurred less to the great principles of morality, than to the records and charters of a barbarous age. As if men were not entitled to all the benefits of the social state, till they could prove their inheriting them from some bequest of their distant progenitors. As if men were not as justifiable and meritorious, in planting liberty in a soil in which it had never existed, as in restoring it where it could be proved only to have suffered a temporary suspension.

The reasons here assigned, strongly tend to evince the necessity of establishing the genuine principles of society, before we enter upon the direct consideration of government. It may be proper in this place to state the fundamental distinction which exists between these topics of enquiry. Men associated at first for the sake of mutual assistance. They did not foresee that any restraint would be necessary, to regulate the conduct of individual members of the society, towards each other, or towards the whole. The necessity of restraint grew out of the errors and perverseness of a few. An acute writer has expressed this idea with peculiar felicity. "Society and government," says he, "are different in themselves, and have different origins. Society is produced by our wants, and government by our wickedness. Society is in every state a blessing; government even in its best state but a necessary evil."

CHAPTER II

OF JUSTICE

CONSIDERABLE light will probably be thrown upon our investigations, if, quitting for the present the political view, we examine justice merely as it exists among individuals. Justice is a rule of conduct originating in the connexion of one percipient being with another. A comprehensive maxim which has been laid down upon the subject is, "that we should love our neighbour as ourselves." But this maxim as a popular principle, is not modelled with the strictness of philosophical accuracy.

In a loose and general view I and my neighbour are both of

us men; and of consequence entitled to equal attention. But, in reality, it is probable that one of us is a being of more worth and importance than the other. A man is of more worth than a beast; because, being possessed of higher faculties, he is capable of a more refined and genuine happiness. In the same manner the illustrious archbishop of Cambray was of more worth than his valet, and there are few of us that would hesitate to pronounce, if his palace were in flames, and the life of only one of them could be preserved, which of the two ought to be preferred.

But there is another ground of preference, beside the private consideration of one of them being further removed from the state of a mere animal. We are not connected with one or two percipient beings, but with a society, a nation, and in some sense with a whole family of mankind. Of consequence that life ought to be preferred which will be most conducive to the general good. In saving the life of Fénelon, suppose at the moment he conceived the project of his immortal Telemachus, I should have been promoting the benefit of thousands, who have been cured by the perusal of that work, of some error, vice and consequent unhappiness. Nay, my benefit would extend further than this, for every individual, thus cured, has become a better member of society, and has contributed in his turn to the happiness, information and improvement of others.

Suppose I had been myself the valet; I ought to have chosen to die, rather than Fénelon should have died. The life of Fénelon was really preferable to that of the valet. But understanding is the faculty that perceives the truth of this and similar propositions; and justice is the principle that regulates my conduct accordingly. It would have been just in the valet to have preferred the archbishop to himself. To have done otherwise would have been a breach of justice.

Suppose the valet had been my brother, my father or my benefactor. This would not alter the truth of the proposition. The life of Fénelon would still be more valuable than that of the valet; and justice, pure, unadulterated justice, would still have preferred that which was most valuable. Justice would have taught me to save the life of Fénelon at the expense of the other. What magic is there in the pronoun 'my,' that should justify us in over-turning the decisions of impartial truth? My brother or my father may be a fool or a profligate, malicious, lying or dishonest. If they be, of what consequence is it that they are mine? . . .

Nothing can be less exposed to reasonable exception than these principles. If there be such a thing as virtue, it must be placed in a conformity to truth, and not to error. It cannot be virtuous, that I should esteem a man, that is, consider him as possessed of estimable qualities, when in reality he is destitute of them. It surely cannot conduce to the benefit of mankind, that each man should have a different standard of moral judgment and preference, and that the standard of all should vary from that of reality. Those who teach this, impose the deepest disgrace upon virtue. They assert in other words, that, when men cease to be deceived, when the film is removed from their eyes, and they see things as they are, they will cease to be either good or happy. Upon the system opposite to theirs, the soundest criterion of virtue is, to put ourselves in the place of an impartial spectator, of an angelic nature, suppose, beholding us from an elevated station, and uninfluenced by our prejudices, conceiving what would be his estimate of the intrinsic circumstances of our neighbour, and acting accordingly.

Having considered the persons with whom justice is conversant, let us next enquire into the degree in which we are obliged to consult the good of others. And here, upon the very same reasons, it will follow, that it is just I should do all the good in my power. Does a person in distress apply to me for relief? It is my duty to grant it, and I commit a breach of duty in refusing. If this principle be not of universal application, it is because, in conferring a benefit upon an individual, I may in some instances inflict an injury of superior magnitude upon myself or society. Now the same justice, that binds me to any individual of my fellow men, binds me to the whole. If, while I confer a benefit upon one man, it appear, in striking an equitable balance, that I am injuring the whole, my action ceases to be right, and becomes absolutely wrong. But how much am I bound to do for the general weal, that is, for the benefit of the individuals of whom the whole is composed? Every thing in my power. To the neglect of the means of my own existence? No; for I am myself a part of the whole. Beside, it will rarely happen that the project of doing for others every thing in my power, will not demand for its execution the preservation of my own existence; or in other words, it will rarely happen that I cannot do more good in twenty years, than in one. If the extraordinary case should occur, in which I can promote the general good by my death more than by my life, justice requires that I should be content to die. In other cases, it will usually be incumbent on me, to maintain my body and mind in the utmost vigour, and in the best condition for service. . . .

But justice is reciprocal. If it be just that I should confer a benefit, it is just that another man should receive it, and, if I withhold from him that to which he is entitled, he may justly complain. My neighbour is in want of ten pounds that I can spare. There is no law of political institution to reach this case, and transfer the property from me to him. But in a passive sense, unless it can be shown that my money can be more beneficially employed, his right is as complete (though actively he have not the same right, or rather duty, to possess himself of it), as if he had my bond in his possession, or had supplied me with goods to the amount. . . .

Society is nothing more than an aggregation of individuals. Its claims and duties, the one no more precarious and arbitrary than the other. What has the society a right to require from me? The question is already answered: everything that it is my duty to do. Any thing more? Certainly not. Can it change eternal truth, or subvert the nature of men and their actions? Can it make my duty consist in committing intemperance, in maltreating or assassinating my neighbour? Again, what is it that the society is bound to do for its members? Everything that is requisite for their welfare. But the nature of their welfare is defined by the nature of mind. That will most contribute to it, which expands the understanding, supplies incitements to virtue, fills us with a generous consciousness of our independence, and carefully removes whatever can impede our exertions.

CHAPTER V

OF RIGHTS

IT is no doubt, the inevitable result of human imperfection, that men and societies of men should model their conduct by the best judgment they are able to form, whether that judgment be sound or erroneous. But as it has been before shown that it cannot be their duty to do anything detrimental to the general happiness, so it appears with equal evidence that they cannot have a right to do so. There cannot be a more absurd proposition, than that which affirms the right of doing wrong. A mistake of this sort, has been attended with the most pernicious consequences in public and political affairs. It cannot be too strongly inculcated, that societies and communities of men are in no case empowered to establish absurdity and injustice; that the voice of the people is not, as has sometimes been ridiculously asserted, "the voice of truth and of God"; and that universal consent cannot convert wrong into right. The most insignificant individual ought to hold himself free to animadvert upon the decisions of the most august assembly; and other men are bound in justice to listen to him, in proportion to the soundness of his reasons, and the strength of his remarks, and not for any accessory advantages he may derive from rank or exterior importance. The most crowded forum, or the most venerable senate, cannot make one proposition to be a rule of justice, that was not substantially so, previously to their decision. They can only interpret and announce that law, which derives its real validity from a higher and less mutable authority. If we submit to their decisions in cases where we are not convinced of their rectitude, this submission is an affair of prudence only; a reasonable man will lament the emergence, while he yields to the necessity. If a congregation of men agree universally to cut off their right hand, to shut their ears upon free enquiry, or to affirm two and two upon a particular occasion to be sixteen, in all cases they are wrong, and ought unequivocally to be censured for usurping an authority that does not belong to them. They ought to be told, "Gentlemen, you are not, as in the intoxication of power you have been led to imagine, omnipotent; there is an authority greater than yours, to which you are bound assiduously to conform yourselves." No man, if he were alone in the world, would have a right to make himself impotent or miserable.

So much for the active rights of man, which, if there be any cogency in the preceding arguments, are all of them superseded and rendered null by their superior claims of justice. His passive rights, when freed from the ambiguity that has arisen from the improper mixture and confounding of these two heads, will probably be found liable to little controversy.

In the first place he is said to have a right to life and personal liberty. This proposition, if admitted, must be admitted with great limitation. He has no right to his life, when his duty calls him to resign it. Other men are bound (it would be improper in strictness of speech, upon the ground of the preceding explanations, to say they have a right) to deprive him of life or liberty, if that should appear in any case to be indispensibly necessary to prevent a greater evil. The passive rights of man will be best understood from the following elucidation.

Every man has a certain sphere of discretion, which he has a right to expect shall not be infringed by his neighbours. This right flows from the very nature of man. First, all men are fallible: no man can be justified in setting up his judgment as a standard for others. We have no infallible judge of controversies; each man in his own apprehension is right in his decisions; and we can find no satisfactory mode of adjusting their jarring pretensions. If every one be desirous of imposing his sense upon others, it will at last come to be a controversy, not of reason, but of force. Secondly, even if we had an infallible criterion, nothing would be gained, unless it were by all men recognised as such. If I were secured against the possibility of mistake, mischief and not good would accrue, from imposing my infallible truths upon my neighbour, and requiring his submission independently of any conviction I could produce in his understanding. Man is a being who can never be an object of just approbation, any further than he is independent. He must consult his own reason, draw his own conclusions, and conscientiously conform himself to his ideas of propriety. Without this, he will be neither active, nor considerate, nor resolute, nor generous.

CHAPTER VI

OF THE RIGHTS OF PRIVATE JUDGMENT

I AM satisfied at present that a certain conduct, suppose it to be a rigid attention to the confidence of private conversation, is incumbent on me. You tell me, "there are certain cases of such peculiar emergency as to supersede this rule." Perhaps I think there are not. If I admit your proposition, a wide field of enquiry is opened, respecting what cases do or do not deserve to be considered as exceptions. It is little likely that we should agree respecting all these cases. How then does the law treat me, for my conscientious discharge of what I conceive to be my duty? Because I will not turn informer (which, it may be, I think an infamous character) against my most valued friend, the law accuses me of misprision of treason, felony, or murder, and perhaps hangs me. I believe a certain individual to be a confirmed villain and a most dangerous member of society, and feel it to be my duty to warn others, perhaps the public, against the effect of his vices. Because I publish what I know to be true, the law convicts me of libel, *scandalum magnatum*, and crimes of I know not what complicated denomination.

If the evil stopped here, it would be well. If I only suffered a certain calamity, suppose death, I could endure it. Death has hitherto been the common lot of men, and I expect, at some time or other, to submit to it. Human society must, sooner or later, be deprived of its individual members, whether they be valuable, or whether they be inconsiderable. But the punishment acts, not only retrospectively upon me, but prospectively upon my contemporaries and countrymen. My neighbour entertains the same opinion respecting the conduct he ought to hold, as I did. The executioner of public justice however interposes with a powerful argument, to convince him that he has mistaken the path or abstract rectitude.

What sort of converts will be produced by this unfeeling logic? "I have deeply reflected," suppose, "upon the nature of virtue, and am convinced that a certain proceeding is incumbent on me. But the hangman, supported by an act of parliament, assures me I am mistaken." If I yield my opinion to his *dictum*, my action becomes modified, and my character also. An influence like this, is inconsistent with all generous magnanimity of spirit, all ardent impartiality in the discovery of truth, and all inflexible perseverance in its assertion. Countries, exposed to the perpetual interference of decrees, instead of arguments, exhibit within their boundaries the mere phantoms of men. We can never judge from an observation of their inhabitants, what men would be, if they knew of no appeal from the tribunal of conscience, and if, whatever they thought, they dared to speak, and dared to act.

BOOK III

Principles of Government

CHAPTER VI

OF OBEDIENCE

THE reason a man lives under any particular government is partly necessity; he cannot easily avoid living under some government, and it is often scarcely in his power to abandon the country in which he was born: it is also partly a choice of evils; no man can be said, in this case, to enjoy that freedom which is essential to the forming a contract, unless it could be shown that he had a power of instituting, somewhere, a government adapted to his own conceptions. Government in reality, as has abundantly appeared, is a question of force, and not of consent. It is desirable, that a government should be made as agreeable as possible to the ideas and inclinations of its subjects; and that they should be consulted, as extensively as may be, respecting its construction and regulations. But, at last, the best constituted government that can be formed, particularly for a large community, will contain many provisions that, far from having obtained the consent of all its members, encounter even in their outset a strenuous, though ineffectual, opposition.—From the whole of these reasonings it appears, that in those measures which have the concurrence of my judgment, I may reasonably be expected to co-operate with willingness and zeal; but, for the rest, my only justifiable ground of obedience is, that I will not disturb the repose of the community, or that I do not perceive the question to be of sufficient magnitude to authorise me in incurring the penalty. . . .

In this view, the best advice that could be given to a person

H

in a state of subjection, is, "Comply, where the necessity of the case demands it; but criticise while you comply. Obey the unjust mandates of your governors; for this prudence and a consideration of the common safety may require; but treat them with no false lenity, regard them with no indulgence. Obey; this might be right; but beware of reverence. Reverence nothing but wisdom and skill: government may be vested in the fittest persons; then they are entitled to reverence, because they are wise, and not because they are governors: and it may be vested in the worst. Obedience will occasionally be right in both cases: you may run south, to avoid a wild beast advancing in that direction, though you want to go north. But be upon your guard against confounding things, so totally unconnected with each other, as a purely political obedience, and respect. Government is nothing but regulated force; force is its appropriate claim upon your attention. It is the business of individuals to persuade; the tendency of concentrated strength, is only to give consistency and permanence to an influence more compendious than persuasion."

All this will be made somewhat clearer, if we reflect on the proper correlative of obedience, authority: and here let us recur to the three sorts of obedience above specified.

The first kind of authority then, is the authority of reason, what is really such, or is only conceived to be such. The terms both authority and obedience are less frequently employed in this sense than in either of the following.

The second species of authority, is that which depends for its validity upon the confidence of him with whom it prevails, and is where, not having myself acquired such information as to enable me to form a judicious opinion, I yield a greater or less degree of deference to the known sentiment and decision of another. This seems to be the strictest and most precise meaning of the word authority; as obedience, in its most refined sense, denotes that compliance which is the offspring of respect.

Authority in the last of the three senses alluded to, is where a man, in issuing his precept, does not deliver that which may be neglected with impunity; but his requisition is attended with a sanction, and the violation of it will be followed with a penalty. This is the species of authority which properly connects itself with the idea of government. It is a violation of political justice, to confound the authority which depends upon force, with the authority which arises from reverence and esteem; the modification of my conduct which might be due in the case of a wild beast, with the modification which is due to superior wisdom. These two kinds of authority may happen to vest in the same person; but they are altogether indistinct and independent of each other.

CHAPTER VII

OF FORMS OF GOVERNMENT

THERE is one other topic relative to general principles of government, which it seems fitting and useful to examine in this place. "Is there a scheme of political institution, which, as coming nearest to perfection, ought to be prescribed to all nations; or, on the other hand, are different forms of government best adapted to the conditions of different nations, each worthy to be commended in its peculiar place, but none proper to be transplanted to another soil?"

The latter part of this alternative is the creed which has ordinarily prevailed; but it is attended with obvious objections.

If one form of government makes one nation happy, why should it not equally contribute to the felicity of another?

The points in which human beings resemble, are infinitely more considerable than those in which they differ. We have the same senses; and the impressions on those senses which afflict me, may ordinarily be expected to be sources of anguish to you. It is true that men differ in their habits and tastes. But these are accidental varieties. There is but one perfection to man; one thing most honourable; one thing that, to a well organised and healthful mind, will produce the most exquisite pleasure. All else is deviation and error; a disease, to be cured, not to be encouraged. Sensual pleasure on the one hand, or intellectual on the other, is, absolutely speaking, the highest and most desirable. We are not to make too much account of the perversions of taste. Men long inured to slavery, for example, undoubtedly have a less exquisite sense of its hatefulness; perhaps instances may be found where it is borne without a murmur. But this is by no means a proof that it is the fit and genuine state of the beings who suffer it. To such men we ought to say, "You are satisfied with an oblivion of all that is eminent in man; but we will awake you. You are contented with ignorance; but we will enlighten you. You are not brutes: you are not stones. You sleep away existence in a miserable neglect of your most valuable privileges: but you are capable of exquisite delights; you are formed to glow with benevolence, to expatiate in the fields of knowledge, to thrill with disinterested transport, to enlarge your thoughts, so as to take in the wonders of the material universe, and the principles that bound and ascertain the general happiness."

If then it appears, that the means which are beneficial to one man, ought, in the most important instances, to be deemed most desirable for others, the same principle which applies to all other sources of moral influence, will also apply to government. Every political system must have a certain influence, upon the moral state of the nation among whom it exists. Some are more favourable, or less inimical, to the general interest, than others. That form of society, which is most conducive to improvement, to the exalted and permanent pleasure of man, the sound politician would wish to see universally realised. . . .

Government, under whatever point of view we examine this

topic, is unfortunately pregnant with motives to censure and complaint. Incessant change, everlasting innovation, seem to be dictated by the true interests of mankind. But government is the perpetual enemy of change. What was admirably observed of a particular system of government, is in a great degree true of all: They "lay their hand on the spring there is in society, and put a stop to its motion." Their tendency is to perpetuate abuse. Whatever was once thought right and useful, they undertake to entail to the latest posterity. They reverse the genuine propensities of man, and, instead of suffering us to proceed, teach us to look backward for perfection. They prompt us to seek the public welfare, not in alteration and improvement, but in a timid reverence for the decisions of our ancestors, as it were the nature of the human mind, always to degenerate, and never to advance.

Man is in a state of perpetual mutation. He must grow either better or worse, either correct his habits or confirm them. The government under which we are placed, must either increase our passions and prejudices by fanning the flame, or, by gradually discouraging, tend to extirpate them. In reality, it is impossible to conceive a government that shall have the latter tendency. By its very nature positive institution has a tendency to suspend the elasticity and progress of mind. Every scheme for embodying imperfection must be injurious. That which is today a considerable melioration, will at some future period, if preserved unaltered, appear a defect and disease in the body politic. It is earnestly to be desired, that each man should be wise enough to govern himself, without the intervention of any compulsory restraint; and, since government, even in its best state, is an evil, the object principally to be aimed at is, that we should have as little of it, as the general peace of human society will permit.

BOOK IV

Of the Operation of Opinion in Societies and Individuals

CHAPTER II

OF REVOLUTIONS

GOVERNMENT is in its nature an expedient, a recourse to something ill to prevent an impending mischief; it affords therefore, no ground of complete satisfaction. Finite things must be perpetually capable of increase and advancement; it would argue therefore extreme folly, to rest in any given state of improvement, and imagine we had attained our summit. The true politician confines neither his expectations nor desires within any specific limits; he has undertaken a labour without end. He does not say, "Let me attain thus much, and I will be contented: I will demand no more; I will no longer counter-act the established order of things: I will set those who support them at rest from further importunity." On the contrary, the whole period of his existence, is devoted to the promotion of innovation and reform.

The direct inference from these sentiments seems to be unfavourable to revolutions. The politician who aims at a limited object, and has shut up his views within that object may be forgiven, if he manifest some impatience for its attainment. But this passion cannot be felt in an equal degree, by him who aims at improvement, not upon a definite, but an indefinite scale. This man knows that, when he has carried any particular point, his task is far from complete. He knows that, when government has been advanced one degree higher in excellence, abuses will still be numerous. Many will be oppressed; many will be exposed to unjust condemnation;

discontent will have its empire and its votaries; and the reign of inequality will be extensive. He can mark therefore the progress of melioration with calmness; though it will have all the wishes of his heart, and all the exertions of his understanding. That progress, which may be carried on, through a longer time, and a greater variety of articles, than his foresight can delineate, he may be expected to desire should take place in a mild and gradual, though incessant advance, not by violent leaps, not by concussions which may expose millions to risk, and sweep generations of men from the stage of existence. . . .

Revolution is instigated by a horror against tyranny, yet its own tyranny is not without peculiar aggravations. There is no period more at war with the existence of liberty. The unrestrained communication of opinions has always been subjected to mischievous counteractions, but upon such occasions it is trebly fettered. At other times men are not so much alarmed for its effects. But in a moment of revolution, when every thing is in crisis, the influence even of a word is dreaded, and the consequent slavery is complete. Where was there a revolution, in which a strong vindication of what it was intended to abolish, was permitted, in indeed almost any species of writing or argument, that was not, for the most part, in harmony with the opinions which happened to prevail? An attempt to scrutinise men's thoughts, and punish their opinions, is of all kinds of despotism the most odious; yet this attempt is peculiarly characteristic of a period of revolution.

The advocates of revolution usually remark, "that there is no way to rid ourselves of our oppressors, and prevent new ones from starting up in their room, but by inflicting on them some severe and memorable retribution." Upon this statement it is particularly observed, that there will be oppressors, as long as there are individuals inclined, either from perverseness, or rooted and obstinate prejudice, to take party with the oppressor. We have therefore to terrify, not only the man of crooked ambition, but all those who would support him, either from a corrupt motive, or a well-intended error. Thus, we propose to make men free; and the method we adopt, is to influence them, more rigorously than ever, by the fear of punishment. We say that government has usurped too much, and we organise a government, tenfold more encroaching in its principles, and terrible in its proceedings. Is slavery the best project that can be devised, for making men free? Is a display of terror the readiest mode, for rendering them fearless, independent and enterprising? . . .

To the remark, that revolutions can scarcely be unaccompanied with the shedding of blood, it may be added that they are necessarily crude and premature. Politics is a science. The general features of the nature of man are capable of being understood, and a mode may be delineated which, in itself considered, is best adapted to the condition of man in society. If this mode ought not, everywhere, and instantly, to be sought to be reduced into practice, the modifications that are to be given it in conformity to the variation of circumstances, and the degrees in which it is to be realised, are also a topic of scientific disquisition. Now it is clearly the nature of science to be progressive in its advances. How various were the stages of astronomy, before it received the degree of perfection which was given it by Newton? How imperfect were the lispings of intellectual science, before it attained the precision of the present century? Political knowledge is, no doubt, in its infancy; and, as it is an affair of life and action, will, in proportion as it gathers vigour, manifest a more uniform and less precarious influence upon the concerns of human society. It is the history of all science to be known first to a few, before it descends through the various descriptions and classes of the community. Thus, for twenty years, the Principia of Newton had scarcely any readers, and his system continued unknown; the next twenty perhaps sufficed to make the outlines of that system familiar, to almost every person, in the slightest degree, tinctured with science.

The only method according to which social improvements can be carried on, with sufficient prospect of an auspicious event, is, when the improvement of our institutions advances, in a just proportion to the illumination of the public understanding. There is a condition of political society best adapted to every different stage of individual improvement. The more nearly this condition is successively realised, the more advantageously will the general interest be consulted. There is a sort of provision in the nature of the human mind for this species of progress. Imperfect institutions, as has already been shown, cannot long support themselves, when they are generally disapproved of, and their effects truly understood. There is a period, at which they may be expected to decline and expire, almost without an effort. Reform, under this meaning of the term, can scarcely be considered as of the nature of action. Men feel their situation; and the restraints that shackled them before, vanish like a deception. When such a crisis has arrived, not a word will need to be drawn, nor a finger to be lifted up in purposes of violence. The adversaries will be too few and too feeble, to be able to entertain a serious thought of resistance against the universal sense of mankind.

Under this view of the subject then it appears, that revolutions, instead of being truly beneficial to mankind, answer no other purpose, than that of marring the salutary and uninterrupted progress, which might be expected to attend upon political truth and social improvement. They disturb the harmony of intellectual nature. They propose to give us something, for which we are not prepared, and which we cannot effectually use. They suspend the wholesome advancement of science, and confound the process of nature and reason.

CHAPTER III

Of Political Associations

ONE of the most obvious features of political association, is its tendency to make a part stand for the whole. A number of persons, sometimes greater and sometimes less, combine together. The tendency of their combination, often avowed, but always unavoidable, is to give to their opinion a weight and operation, which the opinion of unconnected individuals cannot have. A greater number, some from the urgency of their private affairs, some from a temper averse to scenes of concourse and contention, and others from a conscientious disapprobation of the measures pursued, withhold themselves from such combinations. The acrimonious, the intemperate, and the artful, will generally be found among the most forward in matters of this kind. The prudent, the sober, the sceptical, and the contemplative, those who have no resentments to gratify, and no selfish purposes to promote, will be overborne and lost in the progress. What justification can be advanced, for a few persons who thus, from mere impetuosity and incontinence of temper, occupy a post, the very principle of which is, the passing them for something greater and more important in the community than they are? Is the business of reform likely to be well and judiciously conducted in such hands? Add to this, that associations in favour of one set of political tenets, are likely to engender counter-associations in favour of another. Thus we should probably be involved in all the mischiefs of resistance, and all the uproar of revolution.

Political reform cannot be usefully effected, but through the medium of the discovery of political truth. But truth will never be investigated in a manner sufficiently promising, if violence and passion be not removed to a distance. To whatever property adhering to the human mind, or accident affecting it, we are to ascribe the phenomenon, certain it is that truth does not lie upon the surface. It is laborious enquiry, that has, in almost all instances, led to important discovery. If therefore we are desirous to liberate ourselves and our neighbours from the influence of prejudice, we must suffer nothing but arguments to bear sway in the discussion. The writings and the tenets which offer themselves to public attention, should rest upon their own merits. No patronage, no recommendations, no list of venerable names to bribe our suffrage, no importunity to induce us, to bestow upon them our consideration, and to consider them with favour. These however are small matters. It is much worse than this, when any species of publications is patronised by political associations. The publications are then perused, not to see whether what they contain is true or false, but that the reader may learn from them how he is to think upon the subjects of which they treat. A sect is generated, and upon grounds not less irrational, than those of the worst superstition that ever infested mankind. . . .

It follows that the promoting the best interests of mankind, eminently depends upon the freedom of social communication. Let us figure to ourselves a number of individuals, who, having stored their minds with reading and reflection, are accustomed, in candid and unreserved conversation, to compare their ideas, suggest their doubts, examine their mutual difficulties, and cultivate a perspicuous and animated manner of delivering their sentiments. Let us suppose, that their intercourse is not confined to the society of each other, but that they are desirous extensively to communicate the truths with which they are acquainted. Let us suppose their illustrations to be not more distinguished by impartiality and demonstrative clearness, than by the mildness of their temper, and a spirit of comprehensive benevolence. We shall then have an idea of knowledge as perpetually gaining ground, unaccompanied with peril in the means of its diffusion. Their hearers will be instigated to impart their acquisitions to still other hearers, and the circle of instruction will perpetually increase. Reason will spread, and not a brute and unintelligent sympathy.

CHAPTER VII

OF FREE WILL AND NECESSITY

IT remains to turn our attention to the other branch of the subject proposed to be investigated in the present book; the mode in which, from the structure of the human mind, opinion is found to operate in modifying the conduct of individuals. . . .

Of the many controversies which have been excited relative to the operation of opinion, none are of more importance, than the question respecting free will and necessity, and the question respecting self-love and benevolence. These will occupy a principal portion of the enquiry. . . .

To the right understanding of any arguments that may be adduced under this head, it is requisite that we should have a clear idea of the meaning of the term, necessity. He who affirms that all actions are necessary, means that the man, who is acquainted with all the circumstances under which a living or intelligent being is placed upon any given occasion, is qualified to predict the conduct he will hold, with as much certainty, as he can predict any of the phenomena of inaninate nature. Upon this question the advocate of liberty in the philosophical sense, must join issue. He must, if he mean anything, deny this certainty of conjunction between moral antecedents and consequents. Where all is constant and invariable, and the events that arise, uniformly correspond to the circumstances in which they originate, there can be no liberty. . . .

No experiments we are able to make, no reasonings we are able to deduce, can ever instruct us in the principal causation, or show us for what reason it is that one event has, in every instance in which it has been known to occur, been the precursor of another event of a given description. Yet this observation does not, in the slightest degree, invalidate our inference from one event to another, or effect the operations of moral prudence and expectation. The nature of the human mind is such, as to oblige us, after having seen two events perpetually conjoined, to pass, as soon as one of them occurs, to the recollection of the other: and, in cases where this transition never misleads us, but the ideal succession is always found to be an exact copy of the future event, it is impossible that this species of foresight should not be converted into a general foundation of inference and reasoning. We cannot take a single step upon this subject, which does not partake of the species of operation we denominate abstraction. Till we have been led to consider the rising of the sun to-morrow, as an incident of the same species as its rising to-day, we cannot deduce from it similar consequences. It is the business of science to carry this task of generalisation to its furthest extent, and to reduce the diversified events of the universe to a small number of original principles.

Let us proceed to apply these reasonings concerning matter, to the illustration of the theory of mind. Is it possible in this latter theory, as in the former subject, to discover any general principles? Can intellect be made a topic of science? Are we able to reduce the multiplied phenomena of mind to any certain standard of reasoning? If the affirmative of these questions be conceded, the inevitable consequence appears to be, that mind, as well as matter, exhibits a constant conjunction of events, and furnishes all the ground that any subject will afford, for an opinion of necessity. It is of no importance that we cannot see the ground of that necessity, or imagine how sensations, pleasurable or painful, when presented to the mind of a percipient being, are able to generate volition and animal motion; for, if there be any truth in the above statement, we are equally incapable of perceiving a ground of connection between any two events in the material universe, the common and received opinion, that we do perceive such ground of connection, being, in reality, nothing more than a vulgar prejudice. . . .

The idea correspondent to the term character, inevitably includes in it the assumption of necessity and system. The character of any man, is the result of a long series of impressions, communicated to his mind and modifying it in a certain manner, so as to enable us, a number of these modifications and impressions being given, to predict his conduct. Hence arise his temper and habits, respecting which we reasonably conclude, that they will not be abruptly superseded and reversed; and that, if ever they be reversed, it will not be accidentally, but in consequence of some strong reason persuading, or some extraordinary event modifying his mind. If there were not this original and essential conjunction between motives and actions, and between men's past and future actions, there could be no such thing as character, or as a ground of inference, enabling us to predict what men would be, from what they have been.

From the same idea of regularity and conjunction, arise all the schemes of policy, in consequence of which men propose to themselves, by a certain plan of conduct to prevail upon others to become the tools and instruments of their purposes. All the arts of courtship and flattery, of playing upon men's hopes and fears, proceed upon the supposition, that mind is subject to certain laws, and that, provided we be skilful and assiduous enough in applying the motive, the action will inevitably follow.

Lastly, the idea of moral discipline proceeds entirely upon this principle. If I carefully persuade, exhort, and exhibit motives to another, it is because I believe that motives have a tendency to influence his conduct. If I reward or punish him, either with a view to his own improvement, or as an example to others, it is because I have been led to believe that rewards and punishments are calculated to affect the dispositions and practices of mankind.

There is but one conceivable objection, against the inference from these premises to the necessity of human actions. It may be alleged, that "though there is a real coherence between motives and actions, yet this coherence may not amount to a certainty, and, of consequence, the mind still retains an inherent activity, by which it can at pleasure supersede and dissolve it. Thus for example, when I address argument and persuasion to my neighbour, to induce him to adopt a certain species of conduct, I do it not with a certain expectation of success, and am not utterly disappointed if my efforts fail of their object. I make a reserve for a certain faculty of liberty he is supposed to possess, which may at last counteract the best digested projects.". . .

But in this objection there is nothing peculiar to the case of mind. It is just in matter. I see a part only of the premises, and therefore can pronounce only with uncertainty upon the conclusion. A philosophical experiment, which has succeeded a hundred times, may altogether fail in the next trial. But what does the philosopher conclude from this? Not that there is a liberty of choice in his retort and his materials, by which they baffle the best-formed expectations. Not that the established order of antecedents and consequents is imperfect, and that part of the consequent happens without an antecedent. But that there was some other antecedent concerned, to which at the time he failed to advert, but which a fresh investigation will probably lay open to him. When the science of the material universe was in its infancy, men were sufficiently prompt to refer events to accident and chance; but the further they have extended their enquiries and observation, the more reason they have found to conclude, that everything takes place according to necessary and universal laws.

The case is exactly parallel with respect to mind. The

politician and the philosopher, however they may speculatively entertain the opinion of free will, never think of introducing it into their scheme of accounting for events. If an incident turn out otherwise than they expected, they take it for granted, that there was some unobserved bias, some habit of thinking, some prejudice of education, some singular association of ideas, that disappointed their prediction; and, if they be of an active and enterprising temper, they return, like the natural philosopher, to search out the secret spring of this unlooked-for event. . . .

Another argument in favour of the doctrine of necessity, not less clear and irresistible than that from the uniformity of conjunction of antecedents and consequents, will arise from a reference to the nature of voluntary action. The motions of the animal system distribute themselves into two great classes, voluntary and involuntary. "Voluntary action," as we formerly observed, "is, where the event is foreseen, previously to its occurrence, and the hope or fear of that event forms the excitement prompting our effort to forward or retard it."

Here then the advocates of intellectual liberty have a clear dilemma proposed to their choice. They must ascribe this freedom, this imperfect conjunction of antecedents and consequents, either to our voluntary or our involuntary actions. They have already made their determination. They are aware that to ascribe freedom to that which is involuntary, even if the assumption could be maintained, would be altogether foreign to the great subjects of moral, theological or political enquiry. Man would not be in any degree more an agent or an accountable being, though it could be proved that all his involuntary motions sprung up in a fortuitous and capricious manner.

But, on the other hand, to ascribe freedom to our voluntary actions, is an express contradiction in terms. No motion is voluntary, any further than it is accompanied with intention and design, and has for its proper antecedent, the apprehension of an end to be accomplished. So far as it flows, in any degree, from another source, it is involuntary. The new-born infant foresees nothing, therefore all his motions are involuntary. A person arrived at maturity, takes an extensive survey of the consequences of his actions, therefore he is eminently a voluntary and rational being. . . .

It must be unnecessary to add anything further on this head, unless it be a momentary recollection of the sort of benefit that freedom of the will would confer upon us, supposing it possible. Man being, as we have here found him to be, a creature, whose actions flow from the simplest principle, and who is governed by the apprehensions of his understanding, nothing further is requisite but the improvement of his reasoning faculty, to make him virtuous and happy. But did he possess a faculty independent of the understanding, and capable of resisting from mere caprice the most powerful arguments, the best education and the most sedulous instruction might be of no use to him. This freedom we shall easily perceive to be his bane and his curse; and the only hope of lasting benefit to the species, would be, by drawing closer the connection between the external motions and the understanding, wholly to extirpate it. The virtuous man, in proportion to his improve-ment, will be under the constant influence of fixed and in-variable principles; and such a being as we conceive God to be, can never in any one instance have exercised this liberty, that is, can never have acted in a foolish and tyrannical manner. Freedom of the will is absurdly represented as necessary to render the mind susceptible of moral principles; but in reality, so far as we act with liberty, so far as we are independent of motives, our conduct is as independent of morality as it is of reason, nor is it possible that we should deserve either praise or blame for a proceeding thus capricious and indisciplinable.

I

CHAPTER X

OF SELF-LOVE AND BENEVOLENCE

THE enquiry here proposed, is the same in effect, as the question, whether we are capable of being influenced by disinterested considerations. Once admit that we are, and it will not be disputed that it is by such considerations we ought to be influenced, in cases where our neighbour or the public is to be eminently benefited.

This question has been long and eagerly contested, and the majority of persons who are accustomed to give some attention to speculations of this sort, have ranged themselves on the side of self-love. Among the French, not a single writer upon the nature of the human mind, is to be found, who does not, with more or less explicitness, declare for this hypothesis. Among ourselves, several authors of eminence, have undertaken to support the practicability of disinterested action. . . .

An unanswerable argument for the system of disinterestedness, is contained in a proposition so obvious, as for its very plainness to be exposed to the *risque* of contempt, viz. that the motive of every voluntary action, consists in the view present to the mind of the agent at the time of his determination. This is an inference which immediately results from the nature of volition. Volition is an affair of foresight. "No motion is voluntary, any further than it is accompanied with intention and design, and has for its proper antecedent the apprehension of an end to be accomplished. So far as it flows in any degree from another source, it is involuntary." But, if this be a just description of voluntary action, then the converse of this assertion must also be true; that whatever is proposed by the mind as an end to be accomplished, whether it be life or death, pleasure or pain, and relates to myself or my neighbour, has in it the true essence of a motive.—To illustrate this in relation to the subject in hand.

Voluntary action cannot exist but as the result of experience. Neither desire nor aversion can have place, till we have had a consciousness of agreeable and disagreeable sensations. Voluntary action implies desire, and the idea of certain means to be employed for the attainment of the thing desired.

The things first desired by every thinking being will be agreeable sensation, and the means of agreeable sensation. If he foresee any thing that is not apprehended to be pleasure or pain, or the means of pleasure or pain, this will excite no desire, and lead to no voluntary action.

A disposition to promote the benefit of another, my child, my friend, my relation, or my fellow being, is one of the passions; understanding by the term passion, a permanent and habitual tendency towards a certain course of action. It is of the same general nature, as avarice, or the love of fame. The good of my neighbour could not, in the first instance, have been chosen, but as the means of agreeable sensation. His cries, or the spectacle of his distress importune me, and I am irresistibly impelled to adopt means to remove this importunity. The child perceives, in his own case, that menaces or soothing tend to stop his cries, and he is induced to employ, in a similar instance, that mode of the two which seems most within his reach. He thinks little of the sufferings endured, and is only uneasy at the impression made upon his organs. To this motive, he speedily adds the idea of esteem and gratitude, which are to be purchased by his beneficence. Thus the good of our neighbour, like the possession of money, is originally pursued for the sake of its advantage to ourselves.

But it is the nature of the passions, speedily to convert what at first were means into ends. The avaricious man forgets the utility of money which first incited him to pursue it, fixes his passion upon the money itself, and counts his gold, without having in his mind any idea but that of seeing and handling it. Something of this sort happens very early in the history of every passion. The moment we become attached to a particular source of pleasure, beyond any idea we have of the rank it holds in the catalogue of sources, it must be admitted that it is loved for its own sake. The man who pursues wealth or fame with any degree of ardour, soon comes to concentrate his attention in the wealth or the fame, without carrying his mind beyond, or thinking of anything that is to result from them.

This is merely one case of the phenomena of habit. All indulgence of the senses, is originally chosen, for the sake of the pleasure that accrues. But the quantity of accruing pleasure or pain, is continually changing. This, however, is seldom adverted to; and when it is, the power of habit is frequently too strong to be thus subdued. The propensity to do again what we have been accustomed to do, recurs, when the motive that should restrain us has escaped from our thoughts. Thus the drunkard and the lecher continue to pursue the same course of action, long after the pains have outweighed the pleasures, and even after they confess and know this to be the real state of the case. It is in this manner that men will often, for the sake of that which has become the object of a favourite passion, consent to sacrifice what they generally know to contain in it a greater sum of agreeable sensations. It is a trite incontrovertible axiom, "that they will rather die, than part with it."

If this be the case in the passion of avarice or the love of fame, it must also be true in the instance of beneficence, that, after having habituated ourselves to promote the happiness of our child, our family, our country or our species, we are at length brought to approve and desire their happiness without retrospect to ourselves. It happens in this instance, as in the former, that we are occasionally actuated by the most perfect disinterestedness, and willingly submit to tortures and death, rather than see injury committed upon the object of our affections.

Thus far there is a parallel nature in avarice and benevolence. But ultimately there is a wide difference between them. When once we have entered into so auspicious a path as that of disinterestedness, reflection confirms our choice, in a sense in which it never can confirm any of the factitious passions we have named. We find by observation, that we are surrounded by beings of the same nature with ourselves. They have the same senses, are susceptible of the same pleasures and pains, capable of being raised to the same excellence, and employed in the same usefulness. We are able in imagination to go out of ourselves, and become impartial spectators of the system of which we are a part. We can then make an estimate of our intrinsic and absolute value; and detect the imposition of that self-regard, which would represent our own interest as of as much value as that of all the world beside. The delusion being thus sapped, we can, from time to time at least, fall back in idea into our proper post, and cultivate those views and affections which must be most familiar to the most perfect intelligence. . . .

We are capable of self oblivion, as well as of sacrifice. All that is strictly voluntary, in the beneficence of a man habitually generous and kind, commences from this point: if other considerations intervene in the sequel, they are indebted for their intervention to the disinterested motive. But, at the same time that this truth is clearly established, it is not less true, first, that the indirect and original motive, that which laid the foundation of all our habits, is the love of agreeable sensation. Secondly, it is also to be admitted, that there is probably something personal directly and perceptibly mixing itself with such of our beneficent actions as are of a sensible duration. We are so accustomed to fix our attention upon agreeable sensation, that we can scarcely fail to recollect, at every interval, the gratitude we shall excite, or the approbation we shall secure, the pleasure that will result to ourselves from our neighbour's well-being, the joys of self-applause, or the uneasiness that attends upon ungratified desire. Yet after every deduction that can be made, the disinterestedness and direct motive, the profit and advantage of our neighbour, seems to occupy the principal place. This is at least the first, often the only, thing in the view of the mind, at the time the action is chosen. It is this from which, by way of eminence, it derives the character of voluntary action.

There is an observation arising in this place, which it seems of some importance to mention. Pure malevolence is the counterpart of disinterested virtue; and almost all the considerations that prove the existence of the one, are of equal avail to prove the existence of the other. It is not enough to say, I choose the pleasure or pain of my neighbour, for the sake of the gratification I have in contemplating it. This only removes the difficulty a single step, and will not account for the phenomenon of habit in either case. Both the one and the other are originally chosen with a view to agreeable sensation; but in both cases the original view is soon forgotten. It is as certain, that there are human beings who take pleasure in shrieks and agony, without a prospect to any thing further or different, as that the miser comes at last to regard his guineas with delight, independently of a recollection of the benefits they may purchase. . . .

There is no doctrine in which the generous and elevated mind rests with more satisfaction than in that of which we are treating. If it be false, it is no doubt incumbent upon us to make the best of the small remnant of good that remains. But it is a discouraging prospect for the moralist, who, when he has done all, has no hope to persuade mankind to one atom of real affection towards any one individual of their species. We may be made indeed the instruments of good, but in a way less honourable, than that in which a frame of wood, or a sheet of paper, may be made the instrument of good. The wood, or the paper, is at least neutral. But we are drawn into the service, with affections of a diametrically opposite direction. When we perform the most benevolent action, it is with a view only to our own advantage, and with the most sovereign and unreserved neglect of that of others. We are instruments of good, in the same manner as bad men are said to be the instruments of providence, even when their inclinations are most refractory to its decrees. In this sense, we may admire the system of the universe, where public utility results from each man's contempt of that utility, and where the most beneficial actions, of those whom we have been accustomed to term the best men, are only instances in which justice and the real merits of the case are most flagrantly violated. But we can think with little complacence of the individuals of whom this universe is composed. It is no wonder that philosophers whose system has taught them to look upon their fellow men as thus perverse and unjust, have been frequently cold in their temper, or narrow in their designs. It is no wonder that Rousseau, the most benevolent of them, and who most escaped the general contagion, has been driven to place perfection of virtue in doing no injury. Neither philosophy, nor morality, nor politics, will ever show like itself, till man shall be acknowledged for what he really is, a being capable of rectitude, virtue and benevolence, and who needs not always be led to actions of general utility, by foreign and frivolous considerations.

The system of disinterested benevolence proves to us, that it is possible to be virtuous, and not merely to talk of virtue; that all which has been said by philosophers and moralists respecting impartial justice, is not an unmeaning rant; and that, when we call upon mankind to divest themselves of selfish and personal considerations, we call upon them for something they are able to practice. An idea like this, reconciles us to our species; teaches us to regard, with enlightened admiration, the men who have appeared to lose the feeling of their personal existence, in the pursuit of general advantage; and gives us reason to expect that, as men collectively advance in science and useful institution, they will proceed more and more to consolidate their private judgment, and their individual will, with abstract justice, and the unmixed approbation of general happiness.

What are the inferences that ought to be made from this doctrine with respect to political institution? Certainly not that the interest of the individual, ought to be made incompatible with the part he is expected to take in the interest of the whole. This is neither desirable, nor even possible. But that social institution needs not despair of seeing men influenced by other and better motives. The true politician is bound to recollect, that the perfection of mind consists in disinterestedness. He should regard it as the ultimate object of his exertions, to induce men to estimate themselves at their just value, and neither to grant to themselves, nor claim from others, a higher consideration than they deserve. Above all, he should be careful not to add vigour to the selfish passions. He should gradually wean men from contemplating their own benefit in all they do, and induce them to view with complacence the advantage that is to result to others. Great mischief, in this respect, has probably been done by those moralists, who think only of stimulating men to good deeds by considerations of frigid prudence and mercenary self-interest, and never apply themselves to excite one generous and magnanimous sentiment of our natures. This has been too much the case with the teachers of religion, even those of them who are most eager in their hostility to religious enthusiasm.

The last perfection of the sentiment here vindicated, consists in that state of mind, which bids us rejoice as fully in the good that is done by others, as if it were done by ourselves.

CHAPTER XI

OF GOOD AND EVIL

GOOD is a general name, including pleasure, and the means by which pleasure is procured. Evil is a general name, including pain, and the means by which pain is produced. Of the two things included in these general names, the first is cardinal and substantive, and second has no intrinsic recommendations, but depends for its value on the other. Pleasure therefore is to be termed an absolute good; the means of pleasure are only relatively good. The same observation may be stated of pain. . . .

The opposers of the Epicurean maxim, were terrified by a consequence which they hastily concluded might be built upon it. If pleasure were the only thing that is worthy to be desired, they thought that every man might reasonably be justified in "walking in the sight of his own eyes," and there would be no longer any rule of human conduct. Each man might say, "Pleasure is the proper object of my pursuit; I best know what pleases me; and therefore, however opposite is the plan of my conduct to your conceptions, it is unreasonable and unjust for you to interfere with me."

An inference the opposite of this, might, with more propriety, have been drawn from the maxim upon which we are descanting. Is "pleasure the only good?" Then have we the most cogent reason for studying pleasure, and reducing it to a science, and not for leaving every man to pursue his own particular taste, which is nothing more than the result of his education, and of the circumstances in which he happens to have been placed, and which by other lessons and circumstances may be corrected.

No man is entitled to complain of my sober and dispassionate expostulation respecting the species of pleasure he thinks proper to pursue, because no man stands alone, and can pursue his private conceptions of pleasure, without affecting, beneficially or injuriously, the persons immediately connected with him, and, through them, the rest of the world. Even if he have persuaded himself that it is his business to pursue his own pleasure, and that he is not bound to attend ultimately to the pleasure of others, yet it may easily be shown that it is, generally speaking, the interest of each individual, that all should form their plan of personal pleasure with a spirit of deference and accommodation to the pleasure of each other.

But putting the circumstances of the action and re-action of men in society out of the question, still there will be a science of pleasure, and it will be idle and erroneous to consider each man separately, and leave each to find his source of pleasure suitable to his particular humour. We have a common nature, and that common nature ought to be consulted. There is one thing, or series of things, that constitutes the true perfection of man.

In the discussions that took place a few years ago, in the English parliament and nation, respecting the slave-trade, the sentiment we are here combating, was used as a topic of argument, by some of those persons who, from certain deplorable prejudices, were able to prevail upon themselves to appear as advocates for this trade. "The slaves in the West Indies," they said, "are contented with their situation, they are not conscious of the evils against which you exclaim; why then should you endeavour to alter their condition?"

The true answer to this question, even granting them their fact, would be: "It is not very material to a man of a liberal and enlarged mind, whether they are contented or no. Are they contented? I am not contented for them. I see in them beings of certain capacities, equal to certain pursuits and enjoyments. It is of no consequence in the question, that they do not see this, that they do not know their own interests and happiness. They do not repine? Neither does a stone repine. That which you mention as a alleviation, finishes in my conception the portrait of their calamity. Abridged as they are of independence and enjoyment, they have neither the apprehension nor spirit of men. I cannot bear to see human nature thus degraded. It is my duty, if I can, to make them a thousand times happier, than they are, or have any conception of being."

It is not difficult to form a scale of happiness. Suppose it to be something like the following.

The first class shall be such as we may perhaps sometimes find, among the labouring inhabitants of the civilized states of Europe. We will conceive a man, working with his hands every day to obtain his subsistence. He rises early to his labour, and leaves off every night weary and exhausted. He takes a tranquil or a boisterous refreshment, and spends the hours of darkness in uninterrupted slumber. He does not quarrel with his wife, oftener than persons of his class regularly do: and his cares are few, as he has scarcely known the pressure of absolute want. He never repines, but when he witnesses luxuries he cannot partake, and that sensation is transient; and he knows no diseases but those which rise from perpetual labour. The range of his ideas is scanty; and the general train of his sensations, comes as near, as the nature of human existence will admit, to the region of indifference. This man is in a certain sense happy. He is happier than a stone.

Our next instance shall be taken from among the men of rank, fortune and dissipation. We will suppose the individual in question to have an advantageous person and a sound constitution. He enjoys all the luxuries of the palate, the choicest viands, and the best-flavoured wines. He takes his pleasures discreetly, so as not, in the pursuit of pleasure, to lose the power of feeling it. He shoots, he hunts. He frequents public places. He sits up late in scenes of gay resort. He rises late. He has just time to ride and dress, before he goes into company again. With a happy flow of spirits and a perpetual variety of amusements, he is almost a stranger to *ennui*. But he is a model of ignorance. He never reads, and knows nothing beyond the topic of the day. He can scarcely conceive the meaning of the sublime or pathetic; and he rarely thinks of anything beyond himself. This man is happier than the peasant. He is happier, by all the pleasures of the palate, and all the gratifications of neatness, elegance and splendour, in himself, and the objects around him. Every day he is alive, inventing some new amusement, or enjoying it. He takes the pleasures of liberty; he is familiar with the gratifications of pride: while the peasant slides through life, with something of the contemptible insensibility of an oyster.

The man of taste and liberal accomplishments, is more advantageously circumstanced than he whom we have last described. We will suppose him to possess as many of the gratifications of expense as he desires. But, in addition to these, like the mere man of fortune in comparison with the peasant, he acquires new senses, and a new range of enjoyment. The beauties of nature are all his own. He admires the overhanging cliff, the wide extended prospect, the vast expanse of the ocean, the foliage of the woods, the sloping lawn and the waving grass. He knows the pleasures of solitude, when man holds commerce alone with the tranquil solemnity of nature. He has traced the structure of the universe; the substance which compose the globe we inhabit, and are the materials of human industry; and the laws which hold the planets in their course amidst the trackless fields of space. He studies; and has experienced the pleasures which result from conscious perspicacity and discovered truth. He enters, with a true relish, into the sublime and pathetic. He partakes in all the grandeur and enthusiasm of poetry. He is perhaps himself a poet. He is conscious that he has not lived in vain, and that he shall be recollected with pleasure, and extolled with ardour, by generations yet unborn. In this person, compared with the two preceding classes, we acknowledge something of the features of man. They were only a better sort of brutes; but he has sensations and transports of which they have no conception.

But there is a rank of man, more fitted to excite our emulation than this, the man of benevolence. Study is cold, if it be not enlivened with the idea of the happiness to arise to mankind from the cultivation and improvement of sciences. The sublime and pathetic are barren, unless it be the sublime of true virtue, and the pathos of true sympathy. The pleasures of the mere man of taste and refinement, "play round the head, but come not to the heart." There is no true joy, but in the spectacle and contemplation of happiness. There is no delightful melancholy, but in pitying distress. The man who has once performed an act of exalted generosity, knows that there is no sensation of corporeal or intellectual taste to be compared with this. The man who has sought to benefit nations, rises above the mechanical ideas of barter and exchange. He asks no gratitude. To see that they are benefited, or to believe that they will be so, is its own reward. He ascends to the highest of human pleasures, the pleasures of disinterestedness. He enjoys all the good that mankind possess, and all the good that he perceives to be in reserve for them. No man so truly promotes his own interest, as he that forgets it. No man reaps so copious a harvest of pleasure, as he who thinks only of the pleasures of other men. . . .

It may be worthy of remark, that the support the system of optimism derives from the doctrine of necessity, is of a very equivocal nature. The doctrine of necessity teaches, that each event is the only thing, under the circumstances, that could happen; it would, of consequence, be as proper, upon this system, to say that every thing that happens, is the worst, as that it is the best, that could possibly happen. . . .

All nature swarms with life. This may, in one view, afford an idea of an extensive theatre of pleasure. But unfortunately every animal preys upon his fellow. Every animal, however minute, has a curious and subtle structure, rendering him susceptible, as it should seem, of piercing anguish. We cannot move our foot, without becoming the means of destruction. The wounds inflicted are of a hundred kinds. These petty animals are capable of palpitating for days in the agonies of death. It may be said, with little licence of phraseology, that all nature suffers. There is no day nor hour, in which, in some regions of the many-peopled globe, thousands of men, and millions of animals, are not tortured, to the utmost extent that organised life will afford. Let us turn our attention to our own species. Let us survey the poor; oppressed, hungry, naked, denied all the gratifications of life, and all that nourishes the mind. They are either tormented with the injustice, or chilled into lethargy. Let us view man, writhing under the pangs of disease, or the fiercer tortures that are stored up for him by his brethren. Who is there that will look on, and say, "All this is well; there is no evil in the world?" Let us recollect the pains of the mind; the loss of friends, the rankling tooth of ingratitude, the unrelenting rage of tyranny, the slow progress of justice, the brave and honest consigned to the fate of guilt. Let us plunge into the depth of dungeons. Let us observe youth languishing in hopeless despair, and talents and virtue shrouded in eternal oblivion. The evil does not consist merely in the pain endured. It is the injustice that inflicts it, that gives it its sharpest sting. Malignity, an unfeeling disposition, vengeance and cruelty, are inmates of every climate. As these are felt by the sufferer with peculiar acuteness, so they propagate themselves. Severity begets severity, and hatred engenders hate. The whole history of the human species, taken in one point of view, appears a vast abortion. Man seems adapted for wisdom and fortitude and benevolence. But he has always, through a vast majority of countries, been the victim of ignorance and superstition. Contemplate the physiognomy of the species. Observe the traces of stupidity, of low cunning, of rooted insolence, of withered hope, and narrow selfishness, where the characters of wisdom, independence and disinterestedness, might have been inscribed. Recollect the horrors of war, that last invention of deliberate profligacy for the misery of man. Think of the variety of wounds, the multiplication of anguish, the desolation of countries, towns destroyed, harvests flaming, inhabitants perishing by thousands of hunger and cold.

A sound philosophy will teach us to contemplate this scene without madness. Instructed in its lessons, we shall remember that, though there is much of evil, there is also much of good in the world, much pleasure, as well as much pain. We shall not even pronounce that some small portion of this evil is not relatively not an evil. Above all, we shall be cheered with the thought of brighter prospects and happier times. But the optimist must be particularly rash, who takes upon him to affirm of all this mass of evil without exception, that it is relatively not evil, and that nothing could have happened otherwise than it has happened, without the total being worse than it is.

There is reason to think that the creed of optimism, or an opinion bearing some relation to that creed, has done much harm in the world.

It is calculated to overturn all distinction between virtue and vice. The essential part of these ideas, as has been already observed, consists in the tendency of the actions so denominated with respect to the general good. But, according to the doctrine of optimism, if I do a virtuous action, I contribute to the general good; and, if I do a vicious action, it is still the same. Every man, according to this system, is privileged, as the elect are privileged according to the system of certain religionists, "he may live as he list, for he cannot commit sin." Whether I murder my benefactor, or preserve him from being murdered by another, I still do the very best thing that could have been done or thought of.

BOOK V

CHAPTER I

INTRODUCTION

IN reviewing these several branches of authority, and considering the persons to whom they may be most properly confided, we cannot perhaps do better, than adopt the ordinary distribution of forms of government, into monarchy, aristocracy and democracy. Under each of these heads we may enquire into the merits of their respective principles, first absolutely, and upon the hypothesis of their standing singly for the whole administration; and secondly, in a limited view, upon the supposition of their constituting one branch only of the system of government. It is usually alike incident to them all, to confide the minuter branches of executive detail to inferior agents.

One thing more it is necessary to premise. The merits of each of the three heads I have enumerated, are to be considered negatively. The corporate duties of mankind, are the result of their irregularities and follies in their individual capacity. If they had no imperfection, or if men were so constituted, as to be sufficiently, and sufficiently early, corrected by persuasion alone, society would cease from its functions. Of consequence, of the three forms of government, and their compositions, that is the best, which shall least impede the activity and application of our intellectual powers. It was in the recollection of this truth that I have preferred the term political institution to that of government, the former appearing to be sufficiently expressive of that relative form, whatever it be, into which individuals would fall, when there was no need of force to direct them into their proper channel, and were no refractory members to correct.

CHAPTER IV

OF A VIRTUOUS DESPOTISM

MONARCHY, instead of referring every question to the persons concerned or their neighbours, refers it to a single individual, placed at the greatest distance possible from the ordinary members of the society. Instead of distributing the causes to be judged, into as many parcels as convenience would admit, for the sake of providing leisure and opportunities of examination, it draws them to a single centre, and renders enquiry and examination impossible. A despot, however virtuously disposed, is obliged to act in the dark, to derive his knowledge from other men's information, and to execute his decisions by other men's instrumentality. Monarchy seems to be a species of government proscribed by the nature of man; and those persons, who furnished their despot with integrity and virtue, forgot to add omniscience and omnipotence, qualities not less necessary to fit him for the office they had provided. . . .

CHAPTER VIII

OF LIMITED MONARCHY

IN a limited monarchy, there are checks, one branch of the government counteracting the excesses of another, and a check without responsibility, is the most flagrant contradiction. . . .

It was a confused feeling of these truths, that introduced into limited monarchies the principle "that the king can do no wrong." Observe the peculiar consistency of this proceeding. Consider what a specimen it affords of plain dealing, frankness and ingenuous sincerity. An individual is first appointed, and endowed with the most momentous prerogatives; and then it is pretended that, not he, but other men, are answerable for the abuse of these prerogatives. This pretence may appear tolerable to men bred among the fictions of law, but justice, truth and virtue, revolt from it with indignation.

Having first invented this fiction, it becomes the business of such constitutions, as nearly as possible, to realise it. A ministry must be regularly formed; they must concert together; and the measures they execute, must originate in their own discretion. The king must be reduced, as nearly as possible, to

K

a cypher. So far as he fails to be completely so, the constitution must be imperfect.

What sort of figure is it that this miserable wretch exhibits in the face of the world? Every thing is, with great parade, transacted in his name. He assumes all the inflated and oriental style which has been already described, and which indeed was, upon that occasion, transcribed from the practice of a limited monarchy. We find him like Pharaoh's frogs, "in our houses, and upon our beds, in our ovens, and our kneading troughs."

Now observe the man himself, to whom all this importance is annexed. To be idle, is the abstract of his duties. He is paid an immense revenue only to hunt and eat, to wear a scarlet robe and a crown. He may not choose any one of his measures. He must listen, with docility, to the consultations of his ministers, and sanction, with a ready assent, whatever they determine. He must not hear any other advisers; for they are his known and constitutional counsellors. He must not express to any man his opinion; for that would be a sinister and inconstitutional interference. To be absolutely perfect, he must have no opinion, but be the vacant and colourless mirror by which theirs is reflected. He speaks; for they have taught him what he should say: he affixes his signature; for they inform him that it is necessary and proper.

A limited monarchy, in the articles we have described, might be executed with great facility and applause, if a king were, what such a constitution endeavours to render him, a mere puppet regulated by pullies and wires. But it is among the most egregious and palpable of all political mistakes, to imagine that we can reduce a human being to this neutrality and torpor. He will not exert any useful and true activity, but he will be far from passive. The more he is excluded from that energy that characterises wisdom and virtue, the more depraved and unreasonable will he be in his caprices. Is any promotion vacant, and do we expect that he will never think of bestowing it on a favourite, or of proving, by an occasional election of his own, that he really exists? This promotion may happen to be of the utmost importance to the public welfare, or, if not—every promotion unmeritedly given, is pernicious to national virtue, and an upright minister will refuse to assent to it. A king does not fail to hear his power and prerogatives extolled, and he will, no doubt, at some time, wish to essay their reality, in an unprovoked war against a foreign nation, or against his own citizens. . . .

Such then is the genuine and uncontrovertible scene of a mixed monarchy. An individual placed at the summit of the edifice, the centre and the fountain of honour, and who is neutral, or must seem neutral in the current transactions of his government. This is the first lesson of honour, virtue and truth, which mixed monarchy reads to its subjects. Next to the king, come his administration, and the tribe of courtiers; men driven by a fatal necessity, to be corrupt, intriguing and venal; selected for their trust by the most ignorant and ill-formed inhabitants of the realm; made solely accountable for measures of which they cannot solely be the authors; threatened, if dishonest, with the vengeance of an injured people; and, if honest, with the surer vengeance of their sovereign's displeasure. Then the rest of the nation, the subjects at large—

Was ever name so fraught with degradation and meanness as this of subjects? I am, it seems, by the very place of my birth, become a subject. A subject I know I ought to be, to the laws of justice; a subject I know I am, to the circumstances and emergencies under which I am placed. But to be the subject of an individual, of a being with the same form, and the same imperfections as myself; how much must the human mind be degraded, how much must its grandeur and independence be emasculated, before I can learn to think of this with patience, with indifference, nay, as some men do, with pride and exultation? Such is the idol that monarchy worships, in lieu of the divinity of truth, and the sacred obligation of public good. It is of little consequence whether we vow fidelity to the king and the nation, or to the nation and the king, so long as the king intrudes himself to tarnish and undermine the true simplicity, the altar of virtue.

Are mere names beneath our notice, and will they produce no sinister influence upon the mind? May we bend the knee before the shrine of vanity and folly without injury? Far otherwise. Mind had its beginning in sensation, and it depends upon words and symbols for the progress of its associations. The truly good man must not only have a heart resolved, but a front erect. We cannot practise abjection, hypocrisy and meanness, without becoming degraded in other men's eyes and in our own. We cannot "bow the head in the temple of Rimmon," without in some degree apostatising from the divinity of truth. He that calls a king a man, will perpetually hear from his own mouth the lesson, that he is unfit for the trust reposed in him: he that calls him by any sublimer appellation, is hastening fast into the grossest and most dangerous errors.

But perhaps "mankind are so weak and imbecile, that it is in vain to expect, from the change of their institutions, the improvement of their character." Who made them weak and imbecile? Previously to human institutions and human society, they had certainly none of this defect. Man, considered in himself, is merely a being capable of impression, a recipient of perceptions. What is there in this abstract character, that precludes him from advancement? We have a faint discovery in individuals at present, of what our nature is capable: why should individuals be fit for so much, and the species for nothing? Is there any thing in the structure of the globe, that forbids us to be virtuous? If not, if nearly all our impressions of right and wrong flow from our intercourse with each other, why may not that intercourse be susceptible of modification and amendment? It is the most cowardly of all systems, that would represent the discovery of truth as useless, and teach us that, when discovered, it is our wisdom to leave the mass of our species in error.

There is, in reality, little room for scepticism respecting the omnipotence of truth. Truth is the pebble in the lake; and, however slowly, in the present case, the circles succeed each other, they will infallibly go on, till they overspread the surface. No order of mankind will for ever remain ignorant of the principles of justice, equality, and public good. No sooner will they understand them, than they will perceive the coincidence of virtue and public good with private interest: nor will any erroneous establishment be able effectually to support itself against general opinion. In this contest sophistry will vanish, and mischievous institutions sink quietly into neglect. Truth will bring down all her forces, mankind will be her army, and oppression, injustice, monarchy and vice, will tumble into common ruin.

CHAPTER XI

MORAL EFFECTS OF ARISTOCRACY

THERE is one thing, more than all the rest, of importance to the well-being of mankind, justice. A neglect of justice is not only to be deplored for the direct evil it produces; it is perhaps still more injurious, by its effects, in perverting the understanding, overturning our calculations of the future, and thus striking at the root of moral discernment, and genuine power and decision of character. . . .

Let us fairly consider, for a moment, what is the amount of injustice included in the institution of aristocracy. I am born, suppose, a Polish prince with an income of £300,000 per annum. You are born a manorial serf, or a Creolian negro, attached to the soil, and transferable, by barter or otherwise, to twenty successive lords. In vain shall be your most generous efforts, and your unwearied industry, to free yourself from the intolerable yoke. Doomed, by the law of your birth, to wait at the gates of the palace you must never enter; to sleep under a ruined, weather-beaten roof, while your master sleeps under canopies of state; to feed on putrified offals, while the world is ransacked for delicacies for his table; to labour, without moderation or limit, under a parching sun, while he basks in perpetual sloth; and to be rewarded at last with the contempt, reprimand, stripes and mutilation. In fact the case is worse than this. I could endure all that injustice or caprice could inflict, provided I possessed, in the resource of a firm mind, the power of looking down with pity on my tyrant, and of knowing that I had within that sacred character of truth, virtue and fortitude, which all his injustice could not reach. But a slave and a serf are condemned to stupidity and vice, as well as to calamity.

CHAPTER XIV

GENERAL FEATURES OF DEMOCRACY

DEMOCRACY is a system of government, according to which every member of society is considered as a man, and nothing more. So far as positive regulation is concerned, if indeed that can, with any propriety, be termed regulation, which is the mere recognition of the simplest of all moral principles, every man is regarded as equal. Talents and wealth, wherever they exist, will not fail to obtain a certain degree of influence, without requiring positive institution to second their operation. . . .

Supposing that we should even be obliged to take democracy with all the disadvantages that were ever annexed to it, and that no remedy could be discovered for any of its defects, it would still be preferable to the exclusive system of other forms. Let us take. Athens, with all its turbulence and instability; with the popular and temperate usurpations of Pisistrauts and Pericles; with its monstrous ostracism, by which, with undisguised injustice, they were accustomed periodically to banish some eminent citizen, without the imputation of a crime; with the imprisonment of Miltiades, the exile of Aristides, and the murder of Phocion:—with all these errors on its head, it is incontrovertible that Athens exhibited a more illustrious and enviable spectacle, than all the monarchies and aristocracies that ever existed. Who would reject their gallant love of virtue and independence, because it was accompanied with irregularities? Who would pass an unreserved condemnation upon their penetrating mind, their quick discernment, and their ardent feeling, because they were subject occasionally to be intemperate and impetuous. Shall we compare a people of such incredible achievements, such exquisite refinement, gay without insensibility, and splendid without intemperance, in the midst of whom grew up the greatest poets, the noblest artists, the most finished orators, and the most disinterested philosophers, the world ever saw—shall we compare this chosen seat of patriotism, independence, and generous virtue, with the torpid and selfish realms of monarchy and aristocracy? All is not happiness that looks tranquillity. Better were a portion of turbulence and fluctuation, than that unwholesome calm in which all the best faculties of the human mind are turned to putrescence and poison.

In the estimate that is usually made of democracy, one of the sources of our erroneous judgment, lies in our taking mankind such as monarchy and aristocracy have made them, and thence judging how fit they are to manage for themselves. Monarchy and aristocracy would be no evils, if their tendency were not to undermine the virtues and the understandings of their subjects. The thing most necessary, is to remove all those restraints which prevent the human mind from attaining its genuine strength. Implicit faith, blind submission to authority, timid fear, a distrust of our powers, an inattention to our own importance and the good purposes we are able to effect, these are the chief obstacles to human improvement. Democracy restores to man a consciousness of his value, teaches him, by the removal of authority and oppression, to listen only to the suggestions of reason, gives him confidence to treat all other men with frankness and simplicity, and induces him to regard them no longer, as enemies against whom to be upon his guard, but as brethren whom it becomes him to assist. The citizen of a democratic state, when he looks upon the oppression and injustice that prevail in the countries around him, cannot but entertain an inexpressible esteem for the advantages he enjoys, and the most unalterable determination to preserve them. The influence of democracy upon the sentiments of its members, is altogether of the negative sort, but its consequences are inestimable. Nothing can be more unreasonable, than to argue, from men as we now find them, to men as they may hereafter be made. Strict and accurate reasoning, instead of suffering us to be surprised that Athens did so much, would at first induce us to wonder that she retained so many imperfections.

The road to the improvement of mankind, is in the utmost degree simple, to speak and act the truth. If the Athenians had had more of this, it is impossible they should have been so flagrantly erroneous. To express ourselves to all men with honesty and unreserve, and to administer justice without partiality, are principles which, when once thoroughly adopted, are in the highest degree prolific. They enlighten the understanding, give decision to the judgment, and strip misrepresentation of its speciousness. In Athens, men suffered themselves to be dazzled by splendour and show. If the error in their constitution which led to this defect, can be discovered, if a form of political society can be devised, in which men shall be accustomed to judge firmly and soberly, and be habitually exercised to the manliness of truth, democracy will, in that society, cease from the turbulence, instability, fickleness, and violence, that have too often characterised it. Nothing can be more worthy to be depended on, than the omnipotence of truth, or, in other words, than the connection between judgment and the outward behaviour. The contest between truth and falsehood is of itself too unequal, for the former to stand in need of support from any political ally. The more it is discovered, especially that part of it which relates to man in society, the more simple and self-evident will it appear; and it will be found impossible, any otherwise to account for its having been so long concealed, than from the pernicious influence of positive institution.

There is another obvious consideration, that has frequently been alleged to account for the imperfection of ancient democracy, which is worthy of our attention, though it be not so important as the argument which has just been stated. The ancients were unaccustomed to the idea of deputed or representative assemblies; and it is reasonable to suppose, that affairs might often be transacted, with the utmost order, in such assemblies, which might be productive of much tumult and confusion of the citizens at large. By this happy expedient, we secure many of the pretended benefits of aristocracy, as well as the real benefits of democracy. The discussion of national affairs, is brought before persons of superior education and wisdom: we may conceive them, not only the appointed medium of the sentiments of their constituents, but authorised, upon certain occasions, to act on their part, in the same manner as an unlearned parent delegates his authority over his child to a preceptor of greater accomplishments than himself. This idea, within proper limits, might probably be entitled to approbation, provided the elector had the wisdom not to recede from the exercise of his own understanding in political concerns, exerted his censorial power over his representative, and were accustomed, if the representative were unable, after the fullest explanation, to bring him over to his opinion, to transfer his deputation to another.

The true value of the system of representation, seems to be as follows. Large promiscuous assemblies, such as the assemblies of the people in Athens and Rome, must perhaps always be somewhat tumultuous, and liable to many of the vices of democracy enumerated in the commencement of this chapter. A representative assembly, deputed on the part of the multitude, will escape many of their defects. But representative government is necessarily imperfect. It is, as was formerly observed, a point to be regretted, in the abstract notion of civil society, that a majority should overbear a minority, and that the minority, after having opposed and remonstrated, should be obliged practically to submit, to that which was the subject of their remonstrance. But this evil, inseparable from political government, is aggravated by representation, which removed the power of making regulations, one step further from the people whose lot it is to obey them. Representation therefore, though a remedy, or rather a palliative, for certain evils, is not a remedy so excellent or complete, as should authorise us to rest in it, as the highest improvement of which the social order is capable.

CHAPTER XV

OF POLITICAL IMPOSTURE

THERE are disadvantages of no ordinary magnitude that attend upon the practice of political imposture.

It is utterly incompatible with the wholesome tone of the human understanding. Man, we have seen some reason to believe, is a being of progressive nature, and capable of unlimited improvement. But his progress must be upon the plain line of reason and truth. As long as he keeps the open road, his journey is prosperous and promising; but if he turn aside into by-paths, he will soon come to a point, where there is no longer either avenue or track. He that is accustomed to a deceitful medium, will be ignorant of the true colours of things. He that is often imposed on will be no judge of the fair and the genuine. Human understanding cannot be tampered with, with impunity; if we admit prejudice, deception and implicit faith in one subject, the inquisitive energies of the mind will be more or less weakened in all. This is a fact so well known, that the persons who recommend the governing mankind by deception, are, to a man, advocates of the opinion, that the human species is essentially stationary.

A further disadvantage of political imposture, is, that the bubble is hourly in danger of bursting, and the delusion of coming to an end. The playing upon our passions and our imagination, as we have already said, can never fully answer any but a temporary purpose. In delusion there is always inconsistency. It will look plausibly, when placed in a certain light; but it will not bear handling, and examining on all sides. It suits us in a certain animated tone of mind; but in a calm and tranquil season, it is destitute of power. Politics and government are affairs of a durable concern; they should therefore rest upon a basis that will abide the test.

The system of political imposture divides men into two classes, one of which is to think and reason for the whole, and the other to take the conclusions of their superiors on trust. This distinction is not founded in the nature of things; there is no such inherent difference between man and man, as it thinks proper to suppose. Nor is it less injurious, than it is unfounded. The two classes which it creates, must be more and less than man. It is too much to expect of the former, while we consign to them an unnatural monopoly, that they should rigidly consult for the good of the whole. It is iniquitous upon the latter, that they should never employ their understandings, or penetrate into the essences of things, but always rest in a deceitful appearance. It is iniquitous, to deprive them of that chance for additional wisdom, which would result, from a greater number of minds being employed in the enquiry, and from the disinterested and impartial spirit that might be expected to accompany it.

How strangely incongruous is that state of mind, which the system we are here examining, is adapted to recommend. Shall those persons who govern the springs, and carry on the deception, be themselves in the secret of the imposition or not? This is a fundamental question. It has often been started, in relation to the authors or abettors of a new fabric of superstition. On the one hand, we should be apt to imagine, that, for a machine to be guided well, it is desirable that those who guide it, should be acquainted with its principle. We should suppose that, otherwise, the governors we speak of, would not always know the extent and the particulars as to which the deception was salutary; and that, where "the blind led the blind," the public welfare would not be in a much better condition, than the greatest advocates of imposture could suppose it to be under the auspices of truth. But then again, on the other hand, no man can be powerful in persuasion, in a point where he has not first persuaded himself. Beside that the secret must, first or last, be confided to so many hands, that it will be continually in danger of being discovered by the public at large. So that for these reasons it would seem best, that he, who first invented the art of leading mankind at pleasure, and set the wheels of political craft in motion, should suffer his secret to die with him.

And what sort of character must exist in a state thus modified? Those at the head of affairs, if they be acquainted with the principle of the political machine, must be perpetually anxious, lest mankind should unexpectedly recover the use of their faculties. Falsehood must be their discipline and incessant study. We will suppose, that they adopt this system of imposture, in the first instance, from the most benevolent motives. But will the continual practice of concealment, hypocrisy and artifice, make no breaches in their character?

Will they, in despite of habit, retain all that ingenuousness of heart which is the first principle of virtue?

With respect to the multitude, in this system, they are placed in the middle between two fearful calamities, suspicion on one side, and infatuation on the other. Even children, when their parents explain to them, that there is one system of morality for youth, and another for mature age, and endeavour to cheat them into submission, are generally found to suspect the trick. It cannot reasonably be thought, that the mass of the governed in any country, should be less clear sighted than children. Thus they are kept in perpetual vibration, between rebellious discontent, and infatuated credulity. Sometimes they suppose their governors to be the messengers and favourites of heaven, a supernatural order of beings; and sometimes they they suspect them to be a combination of usurpers to rob and oppress them. For they dare not indulge themselves in solving the dilemma, because they are held in awe by oppression and the gallows.

Is this the genuine state of man? Is this a condition so desirable, that we should be anxious to entail it upon posterity for ever? Is it high treason to enquire whether it may be meliorated? Are we sure, that every change from such a situation of things, is severely to be deprecated? Is it not worth while, to suffer that experiment, which shall consist in a gradual, and almost insensible, abolition of such mischievous institutions? . . .

The argument of such a system must, when attentively examined, be the most untenable that can be imagined. It undertakes to prove that we must not be governed by reason. To prove! How prove? Necessarily, from the resources of reason. What can be more contradictory? If I must not trust the conclusions of reason relative to the intrinsic value of things, why trust to your reasons in favour of the benefit of being deceived? You cut off your own argument by the roots. If I must reject the dictates of reason in one point, there can be no possible cause why I should adopt them in another. Moral reasons and inducements, as we have repeatedly shown, consist singly in this, an estimate of consequences. What can supersede this estimate? Not an opposite estimate; for, by the nature of morality, the purpose, in the first instance, is, to take into account all the consequences. Not something else, for a consideration of consequences is the only thing, with which morality and practical wisdom are directly concerned. The moment I dismiss the information of my own eyes and my own understanding, there is, in all justice, an end to persuasion, expostulation or conviction. There is no pretence, by which I can disallow the authority of inference and deduction in one instance, that will not justify a similar proceeding in every other. He that, in any case, designedly surrenders the use of his own understanding, is condemned to remain for ever at the beck of contingence and caprice, and is even bound in consistency, no more to frame his course by the results of demonstration, than by the wildest dreams of delirium and insanity.

CHAPTERS XVIII AND XIX

OF THE CONDUCT OF WAR AND OF MILITARY ESTABLISHMENTS AND TREATIES

It would be unjust, to dismiss the consideration of this most dreadful, yet perhaps, in the present state of things, sometimes unavoidable, calamity, of war, without again reminding the reader of its true character. It is that state of things, where a man stands prepared to deal slaughter and death to his fellow men. Let us imagine to ourselves a human being, surveying, as soon as his appetite for carnage is satiated, the scene of devastation he has produced. Let us view him surrounded with the dying and the dead, his arms bathed to the very elbow in their blood. Let us investigate along with him the features of the field, attempt to divide the wounded from the slain, observe their distorted countenances, their mutilated limbs, their convulsed and palpitating flesh. Let us observe the long-drawn march of the hospital waggons, every motion attended with pangs unutterable, and shrieks that rend the air. Let us enter the hospital itself, and note the desperate and dreadful cases that now call for the skill of the surgeon, even omitting those to which neither skill nor care is ever extended. Whence came all this misery? What manner of creature shall we now adjudge the warrior to be? What had these men done to him? Alas! he knew them not; they had never offended; he smote them to the death, unprovoked by momentary anger, coldly deliberating on faults of which they were guiltless, and executing plans of wilful and meditated destruction. Is not this man a murderer? Yet such is the man who goes to battle, whatever be the cause that induces him. Who that reflects on these things, does not feel himself prompted to say, "Let who will engage in the business of war; never will I, on any pretence, lift up a sword against my brother?" . . .

One branch of the art of war, as well as of every other human art, has hitherto consisted in deceit. If the principles of this work be built upon a sufficiently solid basis, the practice of deceit ought, in almost all instances, to be condemned, whether it proceed from false tenderness to our friends, or from a desire to hasten the downfall of injustice. Vice is neither the most allowable nor effectual weapon, with which to contend against vice. Deceit is certainly not less deceit, whether the falsehood be formed into words, or be conveyed through the medium of fictitious appearances. A virtuous and upright nation, would be scarcely more willing to mislead the enemy, by false intelligence, or treacherous ambuscade, than by the breach of their engagements, or by feigned demonstrations of friendship. There seems to be no essential difference, between throwing open our arms to embrace them, and advancing towards them with neutral colours, or covering ourselves with a defile or a wood. By the practice of surprise and deceipt, we shall oftenest cut off their straggling parties, and shed most blood. By an open display of our force, we shall prevent detachments from being made, and intercept the possibility of supply, without unnecessary bloodshed; and there seems no reason to believe that our ultimate success will be less secure. Why should war be made the science of disingenuousness and mystery, when the plain dictates of good sense would answer all its legitimate purposes? The first principle of defence, is firmness and vigilance. The second perhaps, which is not less immediately connected with the end attained, is frankness and the open disclosure of our purpose, even to our enemies. What astonishment, admiration and terror might this conduct excite in those with whom we had to contend? What confidence and magnanimity would accompany it in our own bosoms? Why should not war, as a step towards its complete abolition, be brought to such perfection, as that the purposes of the enemy might be baffled, without firing a musket, or drawing a sword?

Another corollary, not less inevitable, from the principles which have been delivered, is, that the operations of war should be limited, as accurately as possible, to the generating no further evils, than defence inevitably requires. Ferocity ought carefully to be banished from it. Calamity should, as entirely as possible, be prevented, to every individual who is not actually in arms, and whose fate has no immediate reference to the event of the war. This principle condemns the levying military contributions, and the capture of mercantile vessels. Each of these atrocities would be in another way precluded, by the doctrine of simple defence. We should scarcely think of levying such contributions, if we never attempted to pass the limits of our own territory; and every species of naval war would probably be proscribed.

The utmost benevolence ought to be practised towards our enemies. We should refrain from the unnecessary destruction of a single life, and afford every humane accommodation to the unfortunate. The bulk of those against whom we have to contend, are, comparatively speaking, innocent of the projected injustice. Those by whom it has been most assiduously fostered, are entitled to our kindness as men, and to our compassion as mistaken. It has already appeared, that all ends of punishment are foreign to the transactions of war. It has appeared, that the genuine melioration of war, in consequence of which it may be expected absolutely to cease, is by gradually disarming it of its ferocity. The horrors of war have sometimes been attempted to be vindicated, by a supposition, that the more intolerable it was made, the more quickly would it cease to infest the world. But the direct contrary of this is the truth. Severities beget severities. It is a most mistaken way of teaching men to feel that they are brothers, by imbuing their minds with unrelenting hatred. The truly just man cannot feel animosity, and is therefore little likely to act as if he did.

CHAPTER XXIV

Of the Dissolution of Government

It remains for us to consider, what is the degree of authority necessary to be vested, in such a modified species of national assembly as we have admitted into our system. Are they to issue their commands to the different members of the confederacy? Or is it sufficient, that they should invite them to co-operate for the common advantage, and, by arguments and addresses, convince them of the reasonableness of the measures they propose? The former of these might at first be necessary. The latter would afterwards become sufficient. The Amphictyonic council of Greece possessed no authority, but that which flowed from its personal character. In proportion as the spirit of party was extirpated, as the restlessness of public commotion

L

subsided, and as the political machine became simple, the voice of reason would be secure to be heard. An appeal, by the assembly, to the several districts, would not fail to unite the approbation of reasonable men, unless it contained in it something so evidently questionable, as to make it perhaps desirable that it should prove abortive.[1]

This remark leads us one step further. Why should not the same distinction between commands and invitations, which we have just made in the case of national assemblies, be applied to the particular assemblies or juries of the several districts? At first, we will suppose, that some degree of authority and violence would be necessary. But this necessity does not appear to arise out of the nature of man, but out of the institutions by which he has been corrupted. Man is not originally vicious. He would not refuse to listen to, or to be convinced by, the expostulations that are addressed to him, had he not been accustomed to regard them as hypocritical, and to conceive that, while his neighbour, his parent, and his political governor, pretended to be actuated by a pure regard to his interest or pleasure, they were, in reality, at the expense of his, promoting their own. Such are the fatal effects of mysteriousness and complexity. Simplify the social system, in the manner which every motive, but those of usurpation and ambition, powerfully recommends; render the plain dictates of justice level to every capacity; remove the necessity of implicit faith; and we may expect the whole species to become reasonable and virtuous. It might then be sufficient for juries to recommend a certain mode of adjusting controversies, without assuming the prerogative of dictating that adjustment. It might then be sufficient for them to invite offenders to forsake their errors. If their expostulations proved in a few

---

[1] Godwin's system obviously owes something to that of the newly liberated United States, but the self-governing districts of his confederacy were, of course, to be very much smaller in relation to the whole than any American state, so that each person would be known to the community and subject to the full pressure of public opinion.

instances ineffectual, the evils arising out of this circumstance, would be of less importance, than those which proceed from the perpetual violation of the exercise of private judgment. But, in reality, no evils would arise; for, where the empire of reason was so universally acknowledged, the offender would either readily yield to the expostulations of authority; or, if he resisted, though suffering no personal molestation, he would feel so uneasy, under the unequivocal disapprobation, and observant eye, of public judgment, as willingly to remove to a society more congenial to his errors.

The reader has probably anticipated the ultimate conclusion from these remarks. If juries might at length cease to decide, and be contented to invite, if force might gradually be withdrawn and reason trusted alone, shall we not one day find, that juries themselves, and every other species of public institution, may be laid aside as unnecessary? Will not the reasonings of one wise man, be as effectual as those of twelve? Will not the competence of one individual to instruct his neighbours, be a matter of sufficient notoriety, without the formality of an election? Will there be many vices to correct, and much obstinacy to conquer? This is one of the most memorable stages of human improvement. With what delight must every well-informed friend of mankind look forward, to the auspicious period, the dissolution of political government, of that brute engine, which has been the only perennial cause of the vices of mankind, and which, as has abundantly appeared in the progress of the present work, has mischiefs of various sorts incorporated with its substance, and no otherwise removable than by its utter annihilation!

BOOK VI

Of Opinion considered as a Subject of Political Institution

CHAPTER I

GENERAL EFFECTS OF THE POLITICAL SUPERINTENDENCE OF OPINION

HERE then we perceive, in what manner the purposes of government may be answered, and the independence of the individual suffer the smallest degree of injury. We are shown, how government, which is, in all cases, an evil, may most effectually be limited as to the noxiousness of its influence.

But, if this line be overstepped, if opinion be rendered a topic of political superintendence, we are immediately involved in a slavery, to which no imagination of man can set a termination. The hopes of our improvement are arrested; for government fixes the mercurialness of man to an assigned station. We can no longer enquire or think; for enquiry and thought are uncertain in their direction, and unshackled in their termination. We sink into motionless inactivity and the basest cowardice; for our thoughts and words are beset on every side with penalty and menace. . . .

We shall be still more completely aware of the pernicious tendency of positive institutions, if we proceed explicitly to contrast the nature of mind, and the nature of government. One of the most unquestionable characteristics of the human mind, has appeared to be, its progressive nature. Now, on the other hand, it is the express tendency of positive institution, to retain that with which it is conversant, for ever in the same state. Is then the perfectibility of understanding an attribute of trivial importance? Can we recollect, with coldness and indifference, the advantages with which this quality seems pregnant to the latest posterity? And how are these advantages to be secured? By incessant industry, by a curiosity never to be disheartened or fatigued, by a spirit of enquiry to which a philanthropic mind will allow no pause. The circumstance most indispensibly necessary, is that we should never stand still, that every thing most interesting to the general welfare, wholly delivered from restraint, should be in a state of change, moderate and as it were imperceptible, but continual. Is there any thing that can look with a more malignant aspect upon the general welfare, than an institution tending to give permanence to certain systems and opinions? Such institutions are two ways pernicious; first, which is most material, because they render the future advances of mind inexpressibly tedious and operose; secondly, because, by violently confining the stream of reflection, and holding it for a time in an unnatural state, they compel it at last to rush forward with impetuosity, and thus occasion calamities, which, were it free from restraint, would be found extremely foreign to its nature. If the interference of positive institution had been out of the question, would the progress of intellect, in past ages, have been so slow, as to have struck the majority of ingenuous observers with despair? The science of Greece and Rome upon the subject of politics, was, in many respects, extremely imperfect: yet could we have been so long in appropriating their discoveries, had not the allurements of reward, and the menace of persecution, united to induce us, not to trust to the direct and fair verdict of our own understandings?

CHAPTER II

OF RELIGIOUS ESTABLISHMENTS

ONE of the most striking instances of the injurious effects of the political patronage of opinion, as it at present exists in the world, is to be found in the system of religious conformity. Let us take our example from the church of England, by the constitution of which subscription is required from its clergy, to thirty-nine articles of precise and dogmatical assertion, upon almost every subject of moral and metaphysical enquiry. Here then we have to consider the whole honours and revenues of the church, from the archbishop, who takes precedence next after the princes of the blood royal, to the meanest curate in the nation, as employed in support of a system of blind submission and abject hypocrisy. Is there one man, through this numerous hierarchy, that is at liberty to think for himself? Is there one man among them, that can lay his hand upon his heart, and declare, upon his honour and conscience, that the emoluments of his profession have no effect in influencing his judgment? The supposition is absurd. The most that an honest and discerning man, under such circumstances, can say, is, "I hope not; I endeavour to be impartial."

First, the system of religious conformity, is a system of blind submission. In every country, possessing a religious establishment, the state, from a benevolent care, it may be, for the manners and opinions of its subjects, publicly excites a numerous class of men to the study of morality and virtue. What institution, we might obviously be led to enquire, can be more favourable to public happiness? Morality and virtue are the most interesting topics of human speculation; and the best effects might be expected to result from the circumstance, of many persons perpetually receiving the most liberal education, and setting themselves apart for the express cultivation of these topics. But, unfortunately, these very men are fettered in the outset, by having a code of propositions put into their hands, in a conformity to which all their enquiries must terminate. The direct tendency of science, is to increase from age to age, and to proceed, from the slenderest beginnings, to the most admirable conclusions. But care is taken, in the present case, to anticipate these conclusions, and to bind men, by promises and penalties, not to improve upon the science of their ancestors. The plan is designed indeed to guard against degeneracy and decline; but it makes no provision for advance. It is founded in the most sovereign ignorance of the nature of mind, which never fails to do either the one or the other. . . .

The most malicious enemy of mankind, could not have invented a scheme, more destructive of their true happiness, than that of hiring, at the expense of the state, a body of men, whose business it should seem to be, to dupe their contemporaries into the practice of virtue.

One of the lessons that powerful facts are perpetually reading to the inhabitants of such countries, is that of duplicity and prevarication in an order of men, which, if it exist at all, ought to exist only for reverence. Can it be thought, that this prevarication is not a subject of general notoriety? Can it be supposed, that the first idea that rises to the understanding of the multitude at sight of a clergyman, is not that of a man, who inculcates certain propositions, not so properly because he thinks them true, or thinks them interesting, as because he is hired to the employment? Whatever instruction a code of religious uniformity may fail to convey, there is one that it always communicates, the wisdom of sacrificing our understandings, and maintaining a perpetual discord between our professions and our sentiments. Such are the effects that are produced by political institution, in a case, in which it most zealously intends, with parental care, to guard its subjects from seduction and depravity.

CHAPTER VI

OF LIBELS

IF a veil of partial favour is to be drawn over the indiscretions and faults of mankind, it is easy to perceive whether virtue or vice will be the gainer. There is no terror that comes home to the heart of vice, like the terror of being exhibited to the public eye. On the contrary, there is no reward worthy to be bestowed upon eminent virtue, but this one, the plain, unvarnished proclamation of its excellence in the face of the world.

If the unrestrained discussion of abstract enquiry be of the highest importance to mankind, the unrestrained investigation of character is scarcely less to be cultivated. If truth were universally told of men's dispositions and actions, gibbets and wheels might be dismissed from the face of the earth. The knave unmasked, would be obliged to turn honest in his own defence. Nay, no man would have time to grow a knave. Truth would follow him in his first irresolute essays, and public disapprobation arrest him in the commencement of his career. . . .

At first, it may be, if all restraint upon the freedom of writing and speech were removed, and men were encouraged to declare what they thought, as publicly as possible, every press would be burdened with an inundation of scandal.. But the stories, by their very multiplicity, would defeat themselves. No one man, if the lie were successful, would become the object of universal persecution. In a short time, the reader, accustomed to the dissection of character, would acquire discrimination. He would either detect the imposition by its internal absurdity, or at least would attribute to the story no further weight, than that to which its evidence entitled it.

Libel, like every other human concern, would soon find its level, if it were delivered from the injurious interference of political institution. The libeller, that is, he who utters an unfounded calumny, either invents the story he tells, or delivers it with a degree of assurance, to which the evidence that has offered itself to him, is by no means entitled. In each case he would meet with his proper punishment in the judgment of the world. The consequences of his error would fall back upon himself. He would either pass for a malignant accuser, or for a rash and headlong censurer. Anonymous scandal would be almost impossible, in a state where nothing was concealed. But, if it were attempted, it would be wholly pointless, since, where there could be no honest and rational excuse for concealment, the desire to be concealed, would prove the baseness of the motive.

CHAPTER VIII

OF NATIONAL EDUCATION

THE injuries that result from a system of national education, are, in the first place, that all public establishments include in them the idea of permanence. They endeavour, it may be, to secure and to diffuse whatever of advantageous to society is already known, but they forget that more remains to be known. If they realised the most substantial benefits at the time of their introduction, they must inevitably become less and less useful as they increased in duration. But to describe them as useless, is a very feeble expression of their demerits. They actively restrain the flights of mind, and fix it in the belief of exploded errors. It has frequently been observed of universities, and extensive establishments for the purpose of education, that the knowledge taught there, is a century behind the knowledge, which exists among the unshackled and unprejudiced members of the same political community. The moment any scheme of proceeding gains a permanent establishment, it becomes impressed, as one of its characteristic features, with an aversion to change. Some violent concussion may oblige its conductors to change an old system of philosophy for a system less obsolete; and they are then as pertinaceously attached to this second doctrine, as they were to the first. Real intellectual improvement demands, that mind should, as speedily as possible, be advanced to the height of knowledge already existing among the enlightened members of the community, and start from thence in the pursuit of further acquisitions. But public education has always expended its energies in the supoprt of prejudice; it teaches its pupils, not the fortitude that shall bring every proposition to the test of examination, but the art of vindicating such tenets as may chance to be established. We study Aristotle, or Thomas Aquinas, or Bellarmine, or chief justice Coke, not that we may detect errors but that our minds may be fully impregnated with their absurdities. This feature runs through every species of public establishment; and, even in the petty institution of Sunday schools, the chief lessons that are taught, are a superstitious veneration for the church of England, and to bow to every man in a handsome coat. All this is directly contrary to the true interests of mankind. All this must be unlearned, before we can begin to be wise. . . .

Secondly, the idea of national education, is founded in an inattention to the nature of mind. Whatever each man does for himself, is done well; whatever his neighbours or his country undertake to do for him is done ill. . . .

What I earn, what I acquire only because I desire to acquire it, I estimate at its true value; but what is thrust upon me, may make me indolent, but cannot make me respectable. It is an extreme folly, to endeavour to secure for others, independently of exertion on their part, the means of being happy.—This whole proposition of a national education, is founded upon a supposition which has been repeatedly refuted in this work, but which has recurred upon us in a thousand forms, that unpatronised truth is inadequate to the purpose of enlightening mankind.

Thirdly, the project of a national education ought uniformly to be discouraged, on account of its obvious alliance with national government. This is an alliance of a more formidable nature, than the old and much contested alliance of church and state. Before we put so powerful a machine under the direction of so ambiguous an agent, it behoves us to consider well what it is that we do. Government will not fail to employ it, to strengthen its hands, and perpetuate its institutions. If we could even suppose the agents of government not to propose to themselves an object, which will be apt to appear in their eyes, not merely innocent, but meritorious; the evil would not the less happen. Their views as institutors of a system of education, will not fail to be analogous to their views in their political capacity: the data upon which their conduct as statesmen, is vindicated, will be the data upon which their instructions are founded. It is not true that our youth ought to be instructed to venerate the constitution, however excellent; they should be led to venerate truth; and the constitution only so far as it corresponds with their uninfluenced deductions of truth. Had the scheme of a national education been adopted when despotism was most triumphant, it is not to be believed that it could have for ever stifled the voice of truth. But it would have been the most formidable and profound contrivance for that purpose, that imagination can suggest. Still, in the countries where liberty chiefly prevails, it is reasonably to be assumed that there are important errors, and a national education has the most direct tendency to perpetuate those errors, and to form all minds upon one model.

CHAPTER IX

OF PENSIONS AND SALARIES

LET us proceed to consider the extent of the difficulty that would result from the abolition of salaries. The majority of persons nominated to eminent employments, under any state of mankind approaching to the present, will possess a personal fortune adequate to their support. Those selected from a different class, will probably be selected for extraordinary talents, which will naturally lead to extraordinary resources.

It has been deemed dishonourable to subsist upon private liberality; but this dishonour is produced only by the difficulty of reconciling this mode of subsistence and intellectual independence. It is true that the fortunes of individuals, like public salaries, are merely a patent, empowering them to engross the produce of other men's labour. But large private fortunes cannot cease to exist, till a spirit of sobriety and reflection, hitherto unknown, has been infused into the great mass of mankind. In the mean time the possessors of them are bound to consider the best mode of disposing of their incomes for the public interest: and it would perhaps be difficult to point out a better than that here alluded to. By this method no new addition would be made to the burthens of the laborious; and the distribution would perhaps produce a better effect, than if it were made in douceurs and prizes to the more ordinary classes of mankind. As to the receiver, he, by the supposition, receives no more than his due; and therefore prejudice alone can represent him as degraded, or imbue him with servility. This source of emolument is free from many of the objections that have been urged against a public stipend. I ought to receive your superfluity as my due, while I am employed in affairs more important than that of earning a subsistence; but at the same time to receive it with a total indifference to personal advantage, taking only what I deem necessary for the supply of my wants. He that listens to the dictates of justice, and turns a deaf ear to the suggestions of pride, will probably wish that the customs of his country should cast him for support, on the virtue of individuals, rather than on the public revenue. That virtue may be expected, in this, as in all other instances, to increase, the more it is called into action. . . .

The abolition of salaries, would lead to the abolition of those offices to which salaries are thought necessary. If we had neither foreign wars nor domestic stipends, taxation would be almost unknown; and, if we had no taxes to collect, we should want no clerks to keep an account of them. In the simple scheme of political institution which reason dictates, we could scarcely have any burthensome offices to discharge; and, if we had any that were so in their abstract nature, they might be rendered light by the perpetual rotation of their holders.

BOOK VII

Of Crimes and Punishments

CHAPTER IV

OF THE APPLICATION OF PUNISHMENT

MAN, like every other machine the operations of which can be made the object of our senses, may, in a certain sense, be affirmed to consist of two parts, the external and the internal. The form which his actions assume is one thing; the principle from which they flow is another. With the former it is possible we should be acquainted; respecting the latter there is no species of evidence that can adequately inform us. . . .

But dismissing this difficulty, how complicated is the iniquity of treating all instances alike, in which one man has occasioned the death of another? Shall we abolish the imperfect distinctions, which the most tyrannies have hitherto thought themselves compelled to admit, between chance-medley, manslaughter and malice prepense? Shall we inflict on the man who, endeavouring to save the life of a drowning fellow creature, oversets a boat, and occasions the death of a second, the same suffering, as on him who, from gloomy and vicious habits, is incited to the murder of his benefactor? In reality, the injury sustained by the community, is, by no means, the same in these two cases; the injury sustained by the community, is to be measured by the antisocial dispositions of the offender, and, if that were the right view of the subject, by the encouragement afforded to similar dispositions from his impunity. But this leads us at once, from the external action, to the unlimited consideration of the intention of the actor. The iniquity of the written laws of society, is of precisely the same nature, though not of so atrocious a degree, in the confusion they actually introduce between various intentions, as if this confusion were unlimited. One man shall commit murder, to remove a troublesome observer of his depraved dispositions, who will otherwise counteract and expose him to the world. A second, because he cannot bear the ingenuous sincerity with which he is told of his vices. A third, from his intolerable envy of superior merit. A fourth, because he knows that his adversary meditates an act pregnant with extensive mischief, and perceives no other mode by which its perpetration can be prevented. A fifth, in defence of his father's life or his daughter's chastity. Each of these men, except perhaps the last, may act, either from momentary impulse, or from any of the infinite shades and degrees of deliberation. Would you award one individual punishment to all these varieties of action? Can a system that levels these inequalities, and confounds these differences, be productive of good? That we may render men beneficent towards each other, shall we subvert the very nature of right and wrong?. . . .

But suppose, secondly, that we were to take the intention of the offender, and the future injury to be apprehended, as the standard of infliction. This would no doubt be a considerable improvement. This would be the true mode of reconciling punishment and justice, if, for reasons already assigned, they were not, in their own nature, incompatible. It is earnestly to be desired that this mode of administering retribution should be seriously attempted. It is to be hoped, that men will one day attempt to establish an accurate criterion, and not go on for ever, as they have hitherto done, with a sovereign contempt of equity and reason. This attempt would lead, by a very obvious process, to the abolition of punishment.

It would immediately lead to the abolition of all criminal law. An enlightened and reasonable judicature would have recourse, in order to decide upon the cause before them, to no code but the code of reason. They would feel the absurdity of other men's teaching them what they should think, and pretending to understand the case before it happened, better than they who had all the circumstances under their inspection. They would feel the absurdity of bringing every offence to be compared with a certain number of measures previously invented, and compelling it to agree with one of them. . . .

The great advantage that would result, from men's determining to govern themselves, in the suffering to be inflicted, by the motives of the offender, and the future injury to be apprehended, would consist, in their being taught how vain and presumptuous it is in them to attempt to wield the rod of retribution. Who is it that, in his sober reason, will pretend to assign the motives that influenced me in any article of my conduct, and upon them to found a grave, perhaps a capital, penalty against me? The attempt would be iniquitous and absurd, even though the individual who was to judge me, had made the longest observation of my character, and been most intimately acquainted with the series of my actions. How often does a man deceive himself in the motives of his conduct, and assign to one principle, what, in reality, proceeded from another? Can we expect that a mere spectator should form a judgment sufficiently correct, when he who has all the sources of information in his hands, is nevertheless mistaken?

BOOK VIII

Of Property

CHAPTER I

PRELIMINARY OBSERVATIONS

THE subject of property is the key-stone that completes the fabric of political justice. According as our ideas respecting it are crude or correct, they will enlighten us as to the consequences of a *simple form of society without government*, and remove the prejudices that attach us to complexity. There is nothing that more powerfully tends to distort our *judgment* and *opinions*, than erroneous notions concerning the goods of fortune. Finally, the period that must put an end to the system of *coercion* and *punishment*, is intimately connected with the circumstance of property's being placed upon an equitable basis. . . .

It appears in this respect, as formerly it appeared in the case of our claim to the forbearance of each other, that each man has a sphere, the limit and termination of which is marked out, by the equal sphere of his neighbour. I have a right to the means of subsistence; he has an equal right. I have a right to every pleasure I can participate without injury to myself or others; his title, in this respect is of similar extent.

This view of the subject will appear the more striking, if we pass in review the good things of the world. They may be divided into four classes; subsistence; the means of intellectual and moral improvement; inexpensive gratifications; and such gratifications, as are by no means essential to healthful and vigorous existence, and cannot be purchased but with considerable labour and industry. It is the last class principally that interposes an obstacle in the way of equal distribution.

It will be matter of after-consideration how far and how many articles of this class would be admissible into the purest mode of social existence. But, in the mean time, it is unavoidable to remark the inferiority of this class to the three preceding. Without we may enjoy to a great extent, activity, contentment and cheerfulness. And in what manner are these seeming superfluities usually procured? By abridging multitudes of men, to a deplorable degree, in points of essential moment, that one man may be accommodated, with sumptuous yet, strictly considered, insignificant luxuries.

CHAPTER III

BENEFITS ATTENDANT ON A SYSTEM OF EQUALITY

ACCUMULATED property treads the powers of thought in the dust, extinguishes the sparks of genius, and reduces the great mass of mankind to be immersed in sordid cares; besides depriving the rich, as we have already said, of the most salubrious and effectual motives to activity. If superfluity were banished, the necessity for the greater part of the manual industry of mankind would be superseded; and the rest, being amicably shared among the active and vigorous members of the community, would be burthensome to none. Every man would have a frugal, yet wholesome diet; every man would go forth to that moderate exercise of his corporal functions, that would give hilarity to the spirits; none would be made torpid with fatigue, but all would have leisure to cultivate the kindly and philanthropical affections, and to let loose his faculties in the search of intellectual improvement. What a contrast does this scene present, to the present state of society, where the peasant and the labourer work, till their understandings are benumbed with toil, their sinews contracted and made callous by being for ever on the stretch, and their bodies invaded with

M

infirmities, and surrendered to an untimely grave? What is the fruit they obtain from this disproportioned and unceasing toil? In the evening they return to a family, famished with hunger, exposed half naked to the inclemencies of the sky, hardly sheltered, and denied the slenderest instruction, unless in a few instances, where it is dispensed by the hands of ostentatious charity, and the first lesson communicated is unprincipled servility. . . .

The fruitful source of crimes consists in this circumstance, one man's possessing in abundance, that of which another man is destitute. We must change the nature of mind, before we can prevent it from being powerfully influenced by this circumstance, when brought strongly home to its perceptions by the nature of its situation. Man must cease to have senses, the pleasures of appetite and vanity must cease to gratify, before he can look on tamely at the monopoly of these pleasures. He must cease to have a sense of justice, before he can clearly and fully approve this mixed scene of superfluity and want. It is true, that the proper method of curing this inequality, is by reason and not by violence. But the immediate tendency of the established administration, is to persuade men that reason is impotent. The injustice of which they complain, is upheld by force; and they are too easily induced, by force to attempt its correction. All they endeavour, is the partial correction of an injustice, which education tells them is necessary, but more powerful reason affirms to be tyrannical.

Force grew out of monopoly. It might accidentally have occurred among savages, whose appetites exceeded their supply, or whose passions were inflamed by the presence of the object of their desire; but it would gradually have died away, as reason and civilisation advanced. Accumulated property has fixed its empire; and henceforth all is an open contention, of the strength and cunning of one party, against the strength and cunning of the other. In this case, the violent and premature struggles of the necessitous, are undoubtedly an evil.

They tend to defeat the very cause in the success of which they are most deeply interested; they tend to procrastinate the triumph of justice. But the true crime, in every instance, is in the selfish and partial propensities of men, thinking only of themselves, and despising the emolument of others; and, of these, the rich have their share.

CHAPTER VII

OBJECTIONS TO THIS SYSTEM FROM THE BENEFITS OF LUXURY

THE better to understand the futility of the present objection, it may be proper to enter into a more accurate consideration of the sense of the term luxury. It depends upon the meaning in which it is understood, to determine whether it is to be regarded as a virtue or a vice. If we understand by a luxury, something which is to be enjoyed exclusively by some, at the expense of undue privations, and a partial burthen upon others, to indulge ourselves in luxury is then a vice. But, if we understand by luxury, which is frequently the case, every accommodation which is not absolutely necessary to maintain us in sound and healthful existence, the procuring and communicating luxuries may then be virtuous. The end of virtue, is to add to the sum of pleasurable sensation. The beacon and regulator of virtue, is impartiality, that we shall not give that exertion to procure the pleasure of an individual, which might have been employed in procuring the pleasure of many individuals. Within these limits every man is laudably employed, who procures to himself or his neighbour a real accession of pleasure; and he is censurable, who neglects any occasion of being so employed. We ought not to study that we may live, but to live that we may replenish existence with the greatest number of unallayed, exquisite and substantial enjoyments.

Let us apply these reflections to the state of equality we have endeavoured to delineate. It appeared in that delineation, that the labour of half an hour *per diem* on the part of every individual in the community, would probably be sufficient to procure for all the necessaries of life. This quantity of industry therefore, though prescribed by no law, and enforced by no direct penalty, would be most powerfully imposed upon the strong in intellect, by a sense of justice, and upon the weak, by a sense of shame. After this, how would men spend the remainder of their time? Not probably in idleness, not all men, and the whole of their time, in the pursuit of intellectual attainments. There are many things, the fruit of human industry, which, though not to be classed among the necessaries of life, are highly conducive to our well-being. The criterion of these things will appear, when we have ascertained what those accommodations are which will give us real pleasure, after the insinuations of vanity and ostentation shall have been dismissed. A considerable portion of time would probably be dedicated, in an enlightened community, to the production of such accommodations. A labour of this sort is perhaps not inconsistent with the most desirable state of human existence.

CHAPTER VIII

APPENDIX

OF CO-OPERATION, COHABITATION, AND MARRIAGE

THE subject of cohabitation is particularly interesting, as it includes in it the subject of marriage. It will therefore be proper to pursue the enquiry in greater detail. The evil of marriage, as it is practised in European countries, extends further than we have yet described. The method is, for a thoughtless and romantic youth of each sex, to come together, to see each other, for a few times, and under circumstances full of delusion, and then to vow eternal attachment. What is the consequence of this? In almost every instance they find themselves deceived. They are reduced to make the best of an irretrievable mistake. They are led to conceive it their wisest policy, to shut their eyes upon realities, happy, if by any perversion of intellect, they can persuade themselves that they were right in their first crude opinion of each other. Thus the institution of marriage is made a system of fraud; and men who carefully mislead their judgments in the daily affair of their life, must be expected to have a crippled judgment in every other concern.

Add to this, that marriage, as now understood, is a monopoly, and the worst of monopolies. So long as two human beings are forbidden, by positive institution, to follow the dictates of their own mind, prejudice will be alive and vigorous. So long as I seek, by despotic and artificial means, to maintain my possession of a woman, I am guilty of the most odious selfishness. Over this imaginary prize, men watch with perpetual jealousy; and one man finds his desire, and his capacity to circumvent, as much excited, as the other is excited, to traverse his projects, and frustrate his hopes. As long as this state of society continues, philanthropy will be crossed and checked in a thousand ways, and the still augmenting stream of abuse will continue to flow.

The abolition of the present system of marriage, appears to involve no evils. We are apt to represent that abolition to ourselves, as the harbinger of brutal lust and depravity. But it really happens, in this, as in other cases, that the positive laws which are made to restrain our vices, irritate and multiply them. Not to say, that the same sentiments of justice and happiness, which, in a state of equality, would destroy our relish for expensive gratifications, might be expected to decrease our inordinate appetites of every kind, and to lead us universally to prefer the pleasures of intellect to the pleasures of sense.

It is a question of some moment, whether the intercourse of

the sexes, in a reasonable state of society, would be promiscuous, or whether each man would select himself a partner, to whom he will adhere, as long as that adherence shall continue to be the choice of both parties. Probability seems to be greatly in favour of the latter. Perhaps this side of the alternative is most favourable to population. Perhaps it would suggest itself in preference, to the man who would wish to maintain the several propensities of his frame, in the order due to their relative importance, and to prevent a merely sensual appetite from engrossing excessive attention. It is scarcely to be imagined, that this commerce, in any state of society, will be stripped of its adjuncts, and that men will as willingly hold it, with a woman whose personal and mental qualities they disapprove, as with one of a different description. But it is the nature of the human mind, to persist, for a certain length of time, in its opinion or choice. The parties therefore, having acted upon selection, are not likely to forget this selection when the interview is over. Friendship, if by friendship we understand that affection for an individual which is measured singly by what we know of his worth, is one of the most exquisite gratifications, perhaps one of the most improving exercises, of a rational mind. Friendship therefore may be expected to come in aid of the sexual intercourse, to refine its grossness, and increase its delight. All these arguments are calculated to determine our judgment in favour of marriage as a salutary and respectable institution, but not of that species of marriage, in which there is no room for repentance, and to which liberty and hope are equally strangers.

Admitting these principles therefore as the basis of the sexual commerce, what opinion ought we to form respecting infidelity to this attachment? Certainly no ties ought to be imposed upon either party, preventing them from quitting the attachment, whenever their judgment directs them to quit it. With respect to such infidelities as are compatible with an intention to adhere to it, the point of principal importance is a determination to have recourse to no species of disguise. In ordinary cases, and where the periods of absence are of no long duration, it would seem, that any inconstancy would reflect some portion of discredit on the person that practised it. It would argue that the person's propensities were not under that kind of subordination, which virtue and self-government appear to prescribe. But inconstancy, like any other temporary dereliction, would not be found incompatible with a character of uncommon excellence. What, at present, renders it, in many instances, peculiarly loathsome, is its being practised in a clandestine manner. It leads to a train of falsehood and a concerted hypocrisy, than which there is scarcely any thing that more eminently depraves and degrades the human mind.

The mutual kindness of persons of an opposite sex will, in such a state, fall under the same system as any other species of friendship. Exclusively of groundless and obstinate attachments, it will be impossible for me to live in the world, without finding in one man a worth superior to that of another. To this man I shall feel kindness, in exact proportion to my appreciation of his worth. The case will be the same with respect to the other sex. I shall assiduously cultivate the intercourse of that woman, whose moral and intellectual accomplishments strike me in the most powerful manner. But "it may happen, that other men will feel for her the same preference that I do." This will create no difficulty. We may all enjoy her conversation; and, her choice being declared, we shall all be wise enough to consider the sexual commerce as unessential to our regard. It is a mark of the extreme depravity of our present habits, that we are inclined to suppose the sexual commerce necessary to the advantages arising from the purest friendship. It is by no means indispensible, that the female to whom each man attaches himself in that matter, should appear to each the most deserving and excellent of her sex.

Let us consider the way in which this state of society will

modify education. It may be imagined, that the abolition of
the present system of marriage, would make education, in a
certain sense, the affair of the public; though, if there be any
truth in the reasonings of this work, to provide for it by the
positive institutions of a community, would be extremely
inconsistent with the true principles of an intellectual nature.
Education may be regarded as consisting of various branches.
First, the personal cares which the helpless state of an infant
requires. These will probably devolve upon the mother
unless, by frequent parturition, or by the nature of these cares,
that be found to render her share of the burthen unequal; and
then it will be amicably and willingly participated by others.
Secondly, food and other necessary supplies. These will
easily find their true level, and spontaneously flow, from the
quarter in which they abound, to the quarter that is deficient.
Lastly, the term education may be used to signify instruction.
The task of education, under such a form of society, will be
greatly simplified and altered from what it is at present. It
will then scarcely be thought more necessary to make boys
slaves, than to make men so. The business will not then be, to
bring forward so many adepts in the egg-shell, that the vanity
of parents may be flattered by hearing their praises. No man
will think of vexing with premature learning the feeble and
inexperienced, lest, when they came to years of discretion,
they should refuse to be learned. The mind will be suffered to
expand itself, in proportion as occasion and impression shall
excite it, and not tortured and enervated by being cast in a
particular mould. No creature in human form will be expected
to learn any thing, but because he desires it, and has some
conception of its value; and every man, in proportion to his
capacity, will be ready to furnish such general hints and
comprehensive views, as will suffice for the guidance and
encouragement of him who studies from the impulse of desire.

These observations, lead us to the consideration of one
additional difficulty, which relates to the division of labour.

Shall each man manufacture his tools, furniture and accommodations? This would perhaps be a tedious operation. Every man performs the task to which he is accustomed, more skilfully, and in a shorter time than another. It is reasonable that you should make for me, that which perhaps I should be three or four times as long in making, and should make imperfectly at last. Shall we then introduce barter and exchange? By no means. The moment I require any further reason for supplying you, than the cogency of your claim, the moment, in addition to the dictates of benevolence, I demand a prospect of reciprocal advantage to myself, there is an end of that political justice and pure society of which we treat.

CHAPTER X

REFLECTIONS

To the general mass of the adherents of equality, it may be proper to address a few words. "If there be any force in the arguments of this work, we seem authorised to deduce thus much from them, that truth is irresistible. Let then this axiom be the rudder of our undertakings. Let us not precipitately endeavour to accomplish that today, which the dissemination of truth will make unavoidable tomorrow. Let us not over-anxiously watch for occasions and events: of particular events the ascendancy of truth is independent. Let us anxiously refrain from violence: force is not conviction, and is extremely unworthy of the cause of justice. Let us admit into our bosoms neither contempt, animosity, resentment nor revenge. The cause of justice is the cause of humanity. Its advocates should be penetrated with universal goodwill. We should love this cause; for it conduces to the general happiness of mankind. We should love it; for there is not a man that lives, who, in the natural and tranquil progress of things, will not be made happier by its approach. The most powerful circumstance by which it has been retarded, is the mistake of its adherents, the air of ruggedness, brutishness and inflexibility which they have given to that which, in itself, is all benignity. Nothing less than this could have prevented the great mass of enquirers from bestowing upon it a patient examination. Be it the care of the now increasing advocates of equality, to remove this obstacle to the success of their cause. We have but two plain duties, which, if we set out right, it is not easy to mistake. The first is an unwearied attention to the great instrument of justice, reason. We should communicate our sentiments with the utmost frankness. We should endeavour to press them upon the attention of others. In this we should give way to no discouragement. We should sharpen our intellectual weapons; add to the stock of our knowledge; be pervaded with a sense of the magnitude of our cause; and perpetually add to that calm presence of mind and self-possession which must enable us to do justice to our principles. Our second duty is tranquillity."

It will not be right to pass over a question that will inevitably suggest itself to the mind of the reader. "If an equalisation of conditions be to take place, not by law, regulation or public institution, but only through the private conviction of individuals, in what manner shall it begin?" In answering this question it is not necessary to prove so simple a proposition, as that all republicanism, all reduction of ranks and immunities, strongly tends towards an equalisation of conditions. If men go on to improve in discernment, and this they certainly will with peculiar rapidity, when the ill-constructed governments which now retard their progress are removed, the same arguments which showed them the injustice of ranks, will show them the injustice of one man's wanting that which, while it is in the possession of another, conduces in no respect to his well-being.

It is a **common error** to imagine, "that this injustice will be felt only by the lower orders who suffer from it;" and from thence to conclude "that it can only be corrected by violence." But in answer to this it may, in the first place, be observed that all suffer from it, the rich who engross as well as the poor who want. Secondly, it has been endeavoured to be shown in the course of the present work, that men are not so entirely governed by self-interest, as has frequently been supposed. It appears, if possible, still more clearly, that the selfish are not governed solely by sensual gratification or the love of gain, but that the desire of eminence and distinction is, in different forms, an universal passion. Thirdly and principally, the progress of truth is the most powerful of all causes. Nothing can be more improbable than to imagine, that theory, in the best sense of the word, is not essentially connected with practice. That which we can be persuaded clearly and distinctly to approve, will inevitably modify our conduct. When men shall habitually perceive the folly of individual splendour, and when their neighbours are impressed with a similar disdain, it will be impossible they should pursue the means of it with the same avidity as before.

It will not be difficult to trace, in the progress of modern Europe from barbarism to refinement, a tendency towards the equalisation of conditions. In the feudal times, as now in India and other parts of the world, men were born to a certain station, and it was nearly impossible for a peasant to rise to the rank of a noble. Except the nobles, there were no men that were rich; for commerce, either external or internal, had scarcely an existence. Commerce was one engine for throwing down this seemingly impregnable barrier, and shocking the prejudices of nobles, who were sufficiently willing to believe that their retainers were a different species of beings from themselves. Learning was another, and more powerful engine. In all ages of the church we see men of the basest origin rising to the highest eminence. Commerce proved that others could rise to wealth beside those who were cased in mail; but learning proved that the low-born were capable of surpassing their lords. The progressive effect of these ideas may easily be traced. Long after learning began to unfold its powers, its votaries still submitted to those obsequious manners and servile dedication, which no man reviews at the present day without astonishment. It is but lately that men have known that intellectual excellence can accomplish its purposes without a patron. At present, among the civilised and well informed, a man of slender income, but of great intellectual powers and a firm and virtuous mind, is constantly received with attention and deference; and his purse-proud neighbour who should attempt to treat him superciliously, is sure to encounter a general disapprobation. The inhabitants of distant villages, where long established prejudices are slowly destroyed, would be astonished to see how comparatively small a share wealth has, in determining the degree of attention with which men are treated in enlightened circles.

These no doubt are but slight indications. It is with morality in this respect as it is with politics. The progress is at first so slow as, for the most part, to elude the observation of mankind; nor can it be adequately perceived but by the contemplation and comparison of events during a considerable portion of time. After a certain interval, the scene is more fully unfolded, and the advances appear more rapid and decisive. While wealth was every thing, it was to be expected that men would acquire it, though at the expence of conscience and integrity. The abstract ideas of justice had not yet been so concentrated, as to be able to overpower what dazzles the eye, or promises a momentary gratification. In proportion as the monopolies of rank and corporation are abolished, the value of superfluities will decline. In proportion as republicanism gains ground, men will be estimated for what they are, and not for their accidental appendages.

Let us reflect on the gradual consequences of this revolution of opinion. Liberality of dealing will be among its earliest results; and, of consequence, accumulation will become less frequent and enormous. Men will not be disposed, as now, to take advantage of each other's distresses. They will not consider how much they can extort, but how much it is reasonable to require. The master-tradesman who employs labourers under him, will be disposed to give a more ample regard to their industry; which he is at present enabled to tax, chiefly by the accidental advantage of possessing a capital. Liberality on the part of his employer will complete in the mind of the artisan, what ideas of political justice will probably have begun. He will no longer spend the surplus of his earnings in that dissipation, which is one of the principal of those causes that at present subject him to the arbitrary pleasure of a superior. He will escape from the irresolution of slavery and the fetters of despair, and perceive that independence and ease are scarcely less within his reach than that of any other member of the community. This is an obvious step towards the still further progression, in which the labourer will receive entire whatever the consumer may be required to pay, without having a capitalist, an idle and useless monopoliser, as he will then be found, to fatten upon his spoils.

The same sentiments that lead to liberality of dealing, will also lead to liberality of distribution. The trader, who is unwilling to grow rich by extorting from his customers or his workmen, will also refuse to become rich by the not inferior injustice, of withholding from his indigent neighbour the gratuitous supply of which he stands in need. The habit which was created in the former case of being contented with moderate gains, is closely connected with the habit of being contented with slender accumulation. He that is not anxious to add to his heap, will not be reluctant by a benevolent distribution to prevent its increase. Wealth was at one period almost the single object of pursuit that presented itself to the gross and uncultivated mind. Various objects will hereafter divide men's attention, the love of liberty, the love of equality, the pursuits of art and the desire of knowledge. These objects will not, as now, be confined to a few, but will gradually be laid open to all. The love of liberty obviously leads to a sentiment of union, and a disposition to sympathise in the concerns of others. The general diffusion of truth will be productive of general improvement; and men will daily approximate towards those views according to which every object will be appreciated at its true value. Add to which, that the improvement of which we speak is public, and not individual. The progress is the progress of all. Each man will find his sentiments of justice and rectitude echoed by the sentiments of his neighbours. Apostacy will be made eminently improbable, because the apostate will incur, not only his own censure, but the censure of every beholder.

One objection may perhaps be inferred from these considerations. "If the inevitable progress of improvement insensibly lead towards equality, what need was there of proposing it as a specific object to men's consideration?" The answer to this objection is easy. The improvement in question consists in a knowledge of truth. But our knowledge will be very imperfect, so long as this great branch of universal justice fails to constitute a part of it. All truth is useful; can this truth, which is perhaps the most fundamental of all moral principles, be without its benefit? Whatever be the object towards which mind irresistibly advances, it is of no mean importance to us to have a distinct view of that object. Our advances will thus become accelerated. It is a well known principle of morality, "that he who proposes perfection to himself, though he will inevitably fall short of what he pursues, will make a more rapid progress, than he who is contented to aim only at what is imperfect." The benefits to be derived in the interval from a view of equality as one of the great objects to which we are tending, are exceedingly conspicuous. Such a view will strongly conduce to make us disinterested now. It will teach us to look with contempt upon mercantile speculations, commercial prosperity, and the cares of gain. It will impress us with a just apprehension of what it is of which man is capable, and in which his perfection consists; and will fix our ambition and activity upon the worthiest objects. Intellect cannot arrive at any great and illustrious attainment, however much the nature of intellect may carry us towards it, without feeling some presages of its approach; and it is reasonable to believe that, the earlier these presages are introduced, and the more distinct they are made, the more auspicious will be the event.

III. LITERATURE

NOVELS BY WILLIAM GODWIN

CALEB WILLIAMS IN PRISON

THE whole was a scene of misery, such as nothing short of actual observation can suggest to the mind. Some were noisy and obstreperous, endeavouring by a false bravery to keep at bay the remembrance of their condition; while others, incapable even of this effort, had the torment of their thoughts aggravated by the perpetual noise and confusion that prevailed around them. In the faces of those who assumed the most courage you might trace the furrows of anxious care; and in the midst of their laboured hilarity dreadful ideas would ever and anon intrude, convulsing their features and working every line into an expression of the keenest agony. To these men the sun brought no return of joy. Day after day went on but their state was immutable. Existence was to them a theatre of invariable melancholy; every moment was a moment of anguish, yet did they wish to prolong that moment, fearful that the coming period would bring a severer fate. They thought of the past with insupportable repentance, each man contented to give his right hand to have again the choice of that peace and liberty which he had unthinkingly bartered away. We talk of instruments of torture; Englishmen take credit to themselves for having banished the use of them from their happy shores! Alas, he that has observed the secrets of a prison well knows that there is more torture in the lingering existence of a criminal, in the silent, intolerable minutes that he spends than in the tangible misery of whips and racks.

Such were our days. At sunset our jailors appeared, and

ordered each man to come away and be locked in his dungeon. It was a bitter aggravation of our fate to be under the arbitrary control of these fellows. They felt no man's sorrow; they were of all men least capable of any sort of feeling. They had a barbarous and sullen pleasure in issuing their detested mandates, and observing the mournful reluctance with which they were obeyed. Whatever they directed it was vain to expostulate; fetters and bread and water were the sure consequences of resistance. Their tyranny had no other limit than their own caprice. To whom shall the unfortunate felon appeal? To what purpose complain when his complaints are sure to be received with incredulity? A tale of mutiny and necessary precaution is the unfailing refuge of the keeper, and this tale is an everlasting bar against redress.

Our dungeons were cells $7\frac{1}{2}$ feet by $6\frac{1}{2}$, below the surface of the ground, damp, without window, light or air, except from a few holes worked for that purpose in the door. In some of these miserable receptacles three persons were put to sleep together. I was fortunate enough to have one to myself. It was now the approach of winter. We were not allowed to have candles; and, as I have already said, were thrust in there at sunset and not liberated till the returning day. This was our situation for fourteen or fifteen hours out of the four-and-twenty. I had never been accustomed to sleep more than six or seven hours, and my inclination to sleep was now less than ever. Thus was I reduced to spend half my day in this dreary abode, and in complete darkness. This was no trifling aggravation of my lot.

Among my melancholy reflections I tasked my memory and counted over the doors, the locks, the bolts, the chains, the massy walls, the grated windows that were between me and liberty. "These," said I, "are the engines that tyranny sits down in cold and serious meditation to invent. This is the empire that man exercises over man. Thus is a human being, formed to expatiate, to act, to smile and enjoy, restricted and

N

benumbed. How great must be his depravity or heedlessness, who vindicates this scheme for changing health and gaiety and serenity into the wanness of a dungeon, and the deep furrows of agony and despair!"

"Thank God," exclaims the Englishman, "we have no Bastille! Thank God, with us no man can be punished without a crime!" Unthinking wretch! is that a country of liberty where thousands languish in dungeons and fetters? Go, go ignorant fool! and visit the scenes of our prisons. Witness their unwholesomeness, their filth, the tyranny of their governors, the misery of their inhabitants! After that show me the man shameless enough to triumph, and say that England has no Bastille! Is there any charge so frivolous upon which men are not consigned to these detestable abodes? Is there any villainy that is not practised by justices and prosecutors? But against all this perhaps you have been told there is redress. Yes, a redress that is the consummation of insult so much as to name! Where shall the poor wretch reduced to the last despair, and to whom acquittal perhaps just comes time enough to save him from perishing—where shall this man find leisure, and much less money, to fee officers, and purchase the tedious and dear-bought remedy of the law? No, he is too happy to leave the dungeon and the memory of his dungeon behind him; and the same tyranny and wanton oppression becomes the inheritance of his successor.

For myself I looked round my walls, and forward upon the premature death I had too much reason to expect; I consulted my own heart that whispered nothing but innocence; and I said, "This is society. This is the object, the distribution of justice, which is the end of human reason. For this sages have toiled, and the midnight oil has been wasted. This!" . . .

Thus was I cut off for ever from all that existence has to bestow, from all the high hopes I had so often conceived, from all the future excellence my soul so much delighted to imagine, to spend a few weeks in a miserable prison, and then to perish by the hand of the public executioner. No language can do justice to the indignant and soul-sickening loathing that these ideas excited. My resentment was not restricted to my prosecutor, but extended itself to the whole machinery of human society. I could never believe that all this was the fair result of institutions inseparable from the general good. I regarded the whole human species as so many hangmen and torturers. . . . No man that has not felt in his own most momentous concerns, justice, eternal truth, unalterable equity engaged in his behalf, and on the other side brute force, impenetrable obstinacy, and unfeeling insolence can imagine the sensations that then passed through my mind. I saw treachery triumphant and enthroned; I saw the sinews of innocence crumbled into the dust by the gripe of mighty guilt.

WILLIAM GODWIN, *Caleb Williams* (1794)

CALEB FALLEN AMONG THIEVES

"Comrades, it is for you to decide upon the conduct of this man as you think proper. You know how repeated his offences have been; you know what pains I have taken to amend him. Our profession is the profession of justice—(It is thus that the prejudices of men universally teach them to colour the most desperate cause to which they have determined to adhere).—We, who are thieves without a licence are at open war with another set of men who are thieves according to law. With such a cause then to bear us out, shall we stain it with cruelty, malice and revenge? A thief is, of course, a man living among his equals: I do not pretend therefore to assume any authority among you; act as you think proper; but so far as relations to myself, I vote that Gines be expelled from among us as a disgrace to our society." . . .

The expulsion of this man produced a remarkable improvement in the whole gang. Those who were before inclined to humanity assumed new energy, in proportion as they saw such

sentiments likely to prevail. They had before suffered themselves to be overborne by the boisterous insolence of their
antagonists; but now they adopted, and with success, a
different conduct. Those who envied the ascendance of their
comrade, and therefore, initated his conduct, began to hesitate
in their career. Stories were brought forward of the cruelty
and brutality of Gines, both to men and animals, which had
never before reached the ear of the leader. These stories I shall
not repeat. They could only excite emotions of abhorrence and
disgust, and some of them argued a mind of such a stretch of
depravity as to many readers would appear utterly incredible.
And yet this man had his virtues. He was enterprising,
persevering, and faithful. . . .

Energy is, perhaps, of all qualities the most valuable; and a
just political system would possess the means of extracting
from it, thus circumstanced, its beneficial qualities, instead of
consigning it as now to indiscriminate destruction. We act
like the chymist, who should reject the finest ore, and employ
none but what was sufficiently debased to fit it immediately for
the vilest uses. But the energy of these men, such as I beheld it,
was in the highest degree misapplied, unassisted by liberal and
enlightened views and directed only to the most narrow and
contemptible purposes. . . .

I saw that in this profession were exerted uncommon
energy, ingenuity and fortitude, and I could not help recollec-
ting how admirably beneficial such qualities might be made in
the great theatre of human affairs; while in their present
direction they were thrown away upon purposes diametrically
hostile to the first interests of human society. Nor were their
proceedings less injurious to their own interest than incompatible with the general welfare. The man who risks his life for
the public cause is rewarded with the testimony of an approving
conscience; but those who wantonly defy the necessary, though
atrociously exaggerated precautions of government in the
matter of property, at the same time they commit an alarming

hostility against the whole, are, as to their own concerns, scarcely less absurd and self-neglectful than the man who should set himself up as a mark for a file of musqueteers to shoot at.

Viewing the subject in this light, I not only determined that I would have no share in their occupation myself, but I thought I could not do less, in return for the benefits I had received from them, than endeavour to dissuade them from an employment in which they must themselves be the greatest sufferers. My expostulation met with various reception. All the persons to whom it was addressed had been tolerably successful in persuading themselves of the innocence of their calling, and what remained of doubt in their mind was smothered and, so, to speak, laboriously forgotten. Some of them laughed at my arguments as a ridiculous piece of quixotism. Others, and particularly our captain, repelled them with the boldness of a man that knows he has got the strongest side. But this sentiment of ease and self-satisfaction did not long remain. They had been used to arguments derived from religion and the sacredness of law. They had long ago shaken these from them as so many prejudices. But my view of the subject appealed to principles which they could not contest, and had by no means the air of that customary reproof which is for ever dinned in our ears without finding one responsive chord in our hearts. Finding themselves urged with objections unexpected and cogent, some of those to whom I addressed them began to grow peevish and impatient of the importunate remonstrance. But this was by no means the case with Mr Raymond. He was possessed of a candour I have seldom seen equalled. He was surprised to hear objections so powerful to that which, as a matter of speculation, he believed he had examined on all sides. He revolved them with impartiality and care. He admitted them slowly, but he at length fully admitted them. He had now but one rejoinder in reserve.

"Alas, Williams" said he, "it would have been fortunate for me if these views had been presented to me previously to my embracing my present profession. It is now too late. Those very laws which, by a perception of their iniquity, drove me to what I am now preclude my return. God, we are told, judges of men by what they are at the period of judgement, and whatever be their crimes receives them to favour. But the institutions of countries that profess to worship this God admit no such distinctions. They leave no room for amendment, and seem to have brutal delight in confounding the demerits of offenders. It signifies not what is the character of the individual at the hour of trial. How changed, how spotless, and how useful, avails him nothing. If they discover, at a distance of fourteen,[1] or forty[2] years, an action for which the law ordains that his life shall be forfeit, though the interval should have been spent with the purity of a saint and the devotedness of a patriot, they disdain to enquire into it. What then can I do? Am I not compelled to go on in folly, having once begun?"

WILLIAM GODWIN, *Caleb Williams* (1794)

BACK TO NATURE

Marguerite expostulated with me in the most soothing manner upon the obstinacy of my malady. My Reginald! my love! said she, cease to be unhappy, or to reproach yourself! You were rash in the experiment you made upon the resources of your family. But have you done us mischief or have you conferred a benefit? I more than half incline to the latter opinion. Let us at length dismiss artificial tastes, and idle and visionary pursuits, that do not flow in a direct line from any of the genuine principles of our nature! Here we are surrounded with sources of happiness. Here we may live in true patriarchal

[1] Eugene Aram. See *Annual Register* for 1759.
[2] William Andrew Horne. Ditto, ditto.

simplicity. What is chivalry, what is military prowess and glory? Believe me, they are the passions of a mind depraved, that with ambitious refinement seeks to be wise beyond the dictates of sentiment or reason! There is no happiness so solid or so perfect, as that which disdains these refinements. You, like me, are fond of the luxuriant and romantic scenes of nature. Here [in Switzerland] we are placed in the midst of them. How idle it would be, to wish to change our arbours, our verdant lanes and thickets, for vaulted roofs and gloomy halls, and massy plate? Alas, Reginald! it is I fear too true that the splendour in which we lately lived has its basis in oppression; and that the superfluities of the rich are a boon extorted from the hunger and misery of the poor! Here we see a peasantry more peaceful and less oppressed than perhaps any other tract of the earth can exhibit. They are erect and independent, at once friendly and fearless. Is not this a refreshing spectacle? I now begin practically to perceive that the cultivators of the fields and the vineyards are my brethren and my sisters; and my heart bounds with joy, as I feel my relations to society multiply. How cumbrous is magnificence! The moderate man is the only free. He who reduces all beneath him to a state of servitude, becomes himself the slave of his establishment, and of all his domestics. To diminish the cases in which the assistance of others is felt absolutely necessary, is the only genuine road to independence. We can now move wherever we please without waiting the leisure of others. Our simple repasts require no tedious preparation, and do not imprison us in saloons and eating rooms. Yet we partake of them with a more genuine appetite, and rise from them more truly refreshed than from the most sumptuous feast. I prepare for my meal by industry and exercise; and, when it is over, amuse myself with my children in the fields and the shade.— Though I love the sight of the peasants, I would not be a peasant. I would have a larger stock of ideas, and a wider field of activity. I love the sight of peasants only for their accessories or by comparison. They are comparatively more secure than any other large masses of men, and the scenes in which they are placed are delightful to sense. But I would not sacrifice in prone oblivion the best characteristics of my nature. I put in my claim for refinements and luxuries; but they are the refinements and purifying of the intellect, and the luxuries of uncostly simple state. I would incite the whole world, if I knew how to do it, to put in a similar claim. I would improve my mind; I would enlarge my understanding; I would contribute to the instruction of all about me, and to the mass of human knowledge. The pleasures I would pursue and disseminate, though not dependent on a large property, are such as could not be understood by the rustic and the savage.

WILLIAM GODWIN, *St Leon: A Tale of the Seventeenth Century*
Vol. I, Chapter VII (1799)

THE CUP OF WOE

When he alluded to what he had endured, you did not compassionate him, for you felt he was a creature of another nature; but you confessed that never man seemed to have suffered so much, or to savour with such bitterness the cup of woe. He did not love his wife and children as any other man would do; he probably never dandled or fondled them; his love was speechless. . . . But it brooded over and clung round his heart; and, when it was disturbed, when the strong ties of domestic charity were by the merciless hand of war snapped asunder, you then saw its voluminous folds spread and convulsed before you, gigantic and immeasurable. He cursed their murderers, he cursed mankind, he rose up in fierce defiance of eternal providence; and your blood curdled within you as he spoke. Such was Bethlem Gabor: I could not help admiring him; his greatness excited my wonder and my reverence. . . . There was a similarity in our fortunes that secretly endeared him to me. We had each by the malice of a hostile destiny, though in very different manner, been deprived of our families; we were each of us alone. Fated each to be hereafter for ever alone. . . . Often over our gloomy bowl we mingled groans, and sweetened our draught as we drank it with maledictions.

WILLIAM GODWIN, *St Leon*, Vol. IV, Chapter V (1799)

IN THE SILK FACTORY

I need not tell you that I saw no great expressions of cheerfulness in either the elder or the younger inhabitants of these walls: their occupations were too anxious and monotonous—the poor should not be too much elevated, and incited to forget themselves. There was a kind of stupid and hopeless vacancy in every face: this proceeded from the same causes.

Not one of the persons before me exhibited any signs of vigour or robust health. They were all sallow; their muscles flaccid, and their form emaciated. Several of the children appeared to me judging from their size to be under four years of age—I never saw such children. Some were not tall enough with their little arms to reach the swift; these had stools, which they carried in their hands and mounted as occasion offered. A few, I observed, had a sort of iron buskins on which they were elevated; and, as the iron was worked thin, they were not extremely unwieldy. Children, before they had learned that firm step with the sole of the natural foot, without which it is impossible ever to be a man, were thus disciplined to totter upon stilts. But this was a new invention, and not yet fully established.

This, or nearly all this, I observed upon my first survey of M. Vaublanc's manufactory. In addition to this I afterward found, what you will easily conceive, that it was not without much severity that the children were trained to the regularity I saw. Figure to yourself a child of three or four years of age.

The mind of a child is essentially independent; he does not, until he has been formed to it by hard experience, frame to himself the ideas of authority and subjection. When he is rated by his nurse, he expresses his mutinous spirit by piercing cries; when he is first struck by her in anger, he is ready to fall into convulsions of rage; it almost never happens otherwise. It is a long while (unless he is unmercifully treated indeed) before a rebuke or a blow produces in him immediate symptoms of submission. . . . Almost all that any parent requires of a child of three or four years of age consists in negatives; Stand still: Do not go there: Do not touch that. He scarcely expects or desires to obtain from him any mechanical attention. Contrast this with the situation of the children I saw: brought to the mill at six in the morning; detained till six at night; and, with the exception of half an hour for breakfast, and an hour at dinner, kept incessantly watchful over the safety and regularity of 56 threads continually turning. By my soul, I am ashamed to tell you by what expedients they are brought to this unintermitted vigilance, this dead life, this inactive and torpid industry!

Consider the subject in another light. Liberty is the school of understanding. This is not enough adverted to. Every boy learns more in the hours of play, than in the hours of labour. In school he lays in the materials of thinking; but in his sports he actually thinks: he whets his faculties, and he opens his eyes. The child from the moment of his birth is an experimental philosopher; he essays his organs and his limbs, and learns the use of his muscles. Everyone who will attentively observe him, will find that this is his perpetual employment. But the whole process depends upon liberty. Put him into a mill, and his understanding will improve no more than that of the horse which turns it.

WILLIAM GODWIN, *Fleetwood*, Vol. I, Chapter XI (1805)

MAN ON AN ISLAND

Many were the debates that passed between me and my host respecting the true estimate of the human species. We differed, I suppose first, because we had seen them under unlike circumstances, and in unlike aspects [*i.e.*, those of civilisation and nature]. We differed secondly, because we compared them with different ideal standards. I thought, so to express myself, too highly of the human mind in the abstract, to be able to consider with patience man as he is. I dwelt upon the capacities of our nature, the researches of a Newton, the elevation of a Milton, and the virtues of an Alfred; and, having filled my mind with these, I contemplated even with horror, the ignorance, the brutality, the stupidity, the selfishness, and, as it appeared to me the venality and profligacy in which millions and millions of my fellow-creatures are involved. I estimated mankind, with an eye to the goal which it is ardently to be desired they might reach; Mr MacNeil estimated them with an eye to the starting-post from which they commenced their career. . . . "I have sometimes thought," continued Mr MacNeil, "of composing a little novel or tale in illustration of my position. I would take such a man as my friend Fleetwood, for example, who looks with a disdainful eye upon his species, and has scarcely the patience to enter into discourse and intercourse with anyone he meets: I would put him on board a ship; he will of course be sufficiently disgusted with every one of his companions: all of a sudden I would raise a most furious tempest: I would cause him to be shipwrecked upon a desert island, with no companion but one man, the most gross, perverse and stupid of the crew: all the rest—the captain who, though sagacious, was positive, the surgeon who, though skilful, was tiresome by his pedantry—I would without mercy send to the bottom. What do you think I would represent as the natural result of this situation? My fastidious misanthrope would no longer have a world or a nation, from which to choose his companion. . . . Here, sir, I would show how by degrees he would find a thousand resources in this despised sailor. He would find him active, spirited and alert. Where before he believed, without examination, that all was stupefaction, he would find by a variety of tokens, good sense and sagacity. How these two companions would love one another! How they would occasionally spend the livelong night in delightful chat! How they would study each other's virtues and attainments, even each other's foibles! With what eager anxiety, when any necessary occasion separated them, they would look for each other's return! With what daring and superhuman courage would they defend each other from danger!—And do not be perverse enough to believe that all this anxiety would be the fruit of selfishness! They would have discovered in each other inestimable qualities, a large stock of sound judgement and excellent sense, and an inexhaustible fund of kind and benevolent propensities. After some years I would bring back my misanthrope to England. Sir, he would never be able to part with his companion on the desert isle. He would believe that there was not a creature in the world, take him for all in all, so valuable. Yet observe, he would only entertain this opinion of him, because he knew him more thoroughly than any of the rest of his species. I took my sailor merely as a specimen of human nature, and of human nature in one of its most unfavourable forms."

WILLIAM GODWIN, *Fleetwood*, Vol. I, Chapter XIV (1805)

WRITINGS BY GODWIN'S DISCIPLES

WAR AND TAXES

Hob. Curse on these taxes—one succeeds another—
Our ministers, pandars of a king's will,
Drain all our wealth away, waste it in revels,

And lure, or force away our boys, who should be
The props of our old age, to fill their armies,
And feed the crows of France. Year follows year,
And still we madly prosecute the war;
Draining our wealth, distressing our poor peasants,
Slaughtering our youths—and all to crown our chiefs
With glory!—I detest the hell-sprung name.

    Tyler. What matters me who wears the crown of France?
Whether a Richard or a Charles possess it?
They reap the glory—they enjoy the spoil—
We pay—we bleed! The sun would shine as cheerly,
The rains of heaven as seasonably fall,
Though neither of these royal pests existed.

    Hob. Nay, as for that, we poor men should fare better
No legal robbers then should force away
The hard-earn'd wages of our honest toil.
The Parliament for ever cries *more money*
The service of the state demands more money
Just heaven! of what service is the state? . . .

MINE AND THINE

    Piers. Fare not the birds well, as from spray to spray
Blithesome they bound, yet find their simple food
Scattered abundantly?

    Tyler. No fancied boundaries of mine and thine
Restrain their wanderings. Nature gives enough
For all; but Man, with arrogant selfishness,
Proud of his heaps, hoards up superfluous stores,
Robb'd from his fellows, starves the poor,
Or gives to pity what he owes to justice!

    Piers. So I have heard our good friend John Ball preach.

    Alice. My father, wherefore was John Ball imprison'd?
Was he not charitable, good, and pious?

I have heard him say that all mankind are brethren,
And that like brethren they should love each other;
Was not that doctrine pious?
   Tyler. Rank sedition—
High treason, every syllable, my child!
The priests cry out on him for heresy,
The nobles all detest him as a rebel,
And this good man, this minister of Christ,
This man, the friend and brother of mankind,
Lingers in the dark dungeon!
            ROBERT SOUTHEY, *Wat Tyler*, Act I, Scene I (1794)

SONNET
To William Godwin, Author of "Political Justice"

O form'd t'illumine a sunless world forlorn,
As o'er the chill and dusky brow of Night,
In Finland's wintry skies the Mimic Morn
    Electric pours a stream of rosy light,

Pleas'd I have mark'd OPPRESSION, terror-pale,
    Since, through the windings of her dark machine,
    Thy steady eye has shot its glances keen—
And bade th'All-lovely 'scenes at distance hail.'

Nor will I not thy holy guidance bless,
    And hymn thee, GODWIN! with an ardent lay;
    For that thy voice, in Passion's stormy day,
When wild I roam'd the bleak heath of Distress,

Bade the bright form of Justice meet my way
And told me that her name was HAPPINESS.
SAMUEL TAYLOR COLERIDGE,
    (First published in the *Morning Chronicle*, January 10, 1793)

AN EVIL SOCIETY

Ah far removed from all that glads the sense,
From all that softens or ennobles man,
The wretched many! Bent beneath their loads
They gape at pageant power, nor recognise
Their cots' transmuted plunder! from the tree
Of knowledge, ere the vernal sap had risen,
Rudely disbranched! Evil society!
Fitly depictured by some sun-scorched waste,
Where oft majestic through the tainted noon
The simoon sails, before whose purple pomp
Who falls not prostrate dies! and where, by night,
Fast by each precious fountain on green herbs
The lion couches; or hyaena dips
Deep in the lucid stream his gore-stained jaws;
Or serpent plants his vast moon-glittering bulk,
Caught in whose monstrous twine behemoth yells,
His bones loud-crashing!

SAMUEL TAYLOR COLERIDGE, *Religious Musings* (1794)

TRUTH AND TERROR

57 How weak the solace such fond thoughts afford
When with untimely stroke the virtuous bleed.
Say, rulers of the nations from the sword
Can aught but murder, pain and tears proceed?
Oh what can war but endless war still breed?
Or whence but from the labours of the sage
Can poor benighted mortals gain the meed
Of happiness and virtue, how assuage
But by his gentle words their self-consuming rage?

58 Insensate they who think, at wisdom's porch,
That Exile, Terror, Bonds, and Force may stand;

That Truth with human blood can feed his torch,
And Justice balance with her gory hand
Scales whose dire weight of human heads demand
A Nero's arm. Must Law with its own scourge
Still torture crimes that grew a monstrous band
Formed by his care, and still his victims urge
With voice that breathes despair to death's tremendous
  verge?

61 Heroes of Truth, pursue your march, uptear
The oppressors' dungeon from its deepest base;
High o'er the towers of Pride undaunted rear
Resistless in your might th'Herculean mace
Of Reason, let foul Error's monstrous race
Dragged from their dens start at the light with pain
And die, pursue your toils till not a trace
Be left on earth of Superstition's reign
Save that eternal pile which frowns on Sarum's plain.
    WILLIAM WORDSWORTH, *Guilt and Sorrow*, MS. 1[1] (1794)

THE GODWINIAN MILLENIUM

Mild was the slow necessity of death:
The tranquil spirit failed beneath its grasp,
Without a groan, almost without a fear,
Calm as a voyager to some distant land,
And full of wonder, full of hope as he.
The deadly germs of languor and disease
Died in the human frame, and Purity
Blessed with all gifts her earthly worshippers.
How vigorous then the athletic form of age!
How clear its open and unwrinkled brow!
Where neither avarice, cunning, pride, nor care,
Had stamped the seal of grey deformity
On all the mingling lineaments of time.

    [1] Stanzas omitted from the revised version printed in 1842.

How lovely the intrepid front of youth!
Which meek-eyed courage decked with freshest grace,
Courage of soul, that dreaded not a name,
And elevated will, that journeyed on
Through life's phantasmal scene in fearlessness,
With virtue, love, and pleasure, hand in hand.

Then, that sweet bondage which is Freedom's self,
And rivets with sensation's softest tie
The kindred sympathies of human souls,
Needed no fetters of tyrannic law:
Those delicate and timid impulses
In Nature's primal modesty arose,
And with undoubting confidence disclosed
The growing longings of its dawning love,
Unchecked by dull and selfish chastity,
That virtue of the cheaply virtuous,
Who pride themselves in senselessness and frost.
No longer prostitution's venom'd bane
Poisoned the springs of happiness and life;
Woman and man, in confidence and love,
Equal and free and pure, together trod
The mountain-paths of virtue, which no more
Were stained with blood from many a pilgrim's feet.

Then, where, through distant ages, long in pride
The palace of the monarch-slave had mocked
Famine's faint groan, and Penury's silent tear,
A heap of crumbling ruins stood, and threw
Year after year their stones upon the field,
Wakening a lonely echo; and the leaves
Of the old thorn, that on the topmost tower
Usurped the royal ensign's grandeur, shook
In the stern storm that swayed the topmost tower
And whispered strange tales in the Whirlwind's ear.

O

Low through the lone cathedral's roofless aisles
The melancholy winds a death-dirge sung:
It were a sight of awfulness to see
The works of faith and slavery, so vast,
So sumptuous, yet so perishing withal!
Even as the corpse that rests beneath its wall.
A thousand mourners deck the pomp of death
To-day, the breathing marble glows above
To decorate its memory, and tongues
Are busy of its life; tomorrow worms
In silence and in darkness seize their prey.

Within the massy prison's mouldering courts,
Fearless and free the ruddy children played,
Weaving gay chaplets for their innocent brows
With the green ivy and the red wallflower,
That mock the dungeon's unavailing gloom;
The ponderous chains and gratings of strong iron,
There rusted amid heaps of broken stone
That mingled slowly with their native earth:
There the broad beam of day, which feebly once
Lighted the cheek of lean captivity
With a pale and sickly glare, then freely shone
On the pure smiles of infant playfulness.
No more the shuddering voice of hoarse Despair
Pealed through the echoing vaults, but soothing notes
Of ivy-fingered winds and gladsome birds
And merriment were resonant around.

These ruins soon left not a wreck behind:
Their elements, wide scattered o'er the globe,
To happier shapes were moulded, and became
Ministrant to all blissful impulses:
Thus human beings were perfected, and earth,
Even as a child beneath its mother's love,

Was strengthened in all excellence, and grew
Fairer and nobler with each passing year.
    PERCY BYSSHE SHELLEY, *Queen Mab*, Canto IX (1813)

A NOBLE HOPE

In secret chambers parents read, and weep,
My writings to their babes, no longer blind;
And young men gather when their tyrants sleep,
And vows of faith each to the other bind;
And marriageable maidens, who have pined
With love, till life seemed melting through their look,
A warmer zeal, a nobler hope now find;
And every bosom thus is rapt and shook,
Like autumn's myriad leaves in one swoln mountain-brook.

The tyrants of the Golden City tremble
At voices which are heard about the streets,
The ministers of fraud can scarce dissemble
The lies of their own heart; but when one meets
Another at the shrine, he inly weets,
Though he says nothing, that the truth is known;
Murderers are pale up in the judgement-seats,
And gold grows vile, even to the wealthy crone,
And laughter fills the Fane and curses shake the Throne.

Kind thoughts, and mighty hopes, and gentle deeds
Abound, for fearless love and the pure law
Of mild equality and peace, succeeds
To faiths which long have held the world in awe,
Bloody and false, and cold.
    PERCY BYSSHE SHELLEY, *The Revolt of Islam*, Canto IV (1818)

MAN ALONE

Nor happiness, nor majesty, nor fame
Nor peace, nor strength, nor skill in arms or arts,
Shepherd those herds whom tyranny makes tame;
Verse echoes not one beating of their hearts,
History is but the shadow of their shame,
Art veils her glass, or from the pageant starts
As to oblivion their blind millions fleet,
Staining that heaven with obscene imagery
Of their own likeness. What are numbers knit
By force or custom? Man who man would be,
Must rule the empire of himself; in it
Must be supreme, establishing his throne
On vanquished will, quelling the anarchy
Of hopes and fears, being himself alone.

PERCY BYSSHE SHELLEY, *Political Greatness* (1821)

A MIGHTY CHANGE

As I have said I floated to the earth:
It was, as it is still, the pain of bliss
To move, to breathe, to be; I wandering went
Among the haunts and dwellings of mankind,
And first was disappointed not to see
Such mighty change as I had felt within
Expressed in outward things; but soon I looked,
And behold, thrones were kingless, and men walked
One with the other even as spirits do,
None fawned, none trampled; hate, disdain, or fear,
Self-love or self-contempt, on human brows
No more inscribed, as o'er the gate of hell,
"All hope abandon ye who enter here";
None frowned, none trembled, none with eager fear
Gazed on another's eye of cold command,

Until the subject of a tyrant's will
Became, worse fate, the abject of his own,
Which spurred him, like an outspent horse, to death.
None wrought his lips in truth-entangling lines
Which smiled the lie his tongue disdained to speak;
None, with firm sneer, trod out in his own heart
The sparks of love and hope till there remained
Those bitter ashes, a soul self-consumed,
And the wretch crept a vampire among men,
Infecting all with his own hideous ill;
None talked that common, false, cold, hollow talk
Which makes the heart deny the *yes* it breathes,
Yet question that unmeant hypocrisy
With such a self-mistrust as has no name. . . .

The loathsome mask has fallen, the man remains
Sceptreless, free, uncircumscribed, but man
Equal, unclassed, tribeless, and nationless,
Exempt from awe, worship, degree, the king
Over himself; just, gentle, wise: but man
Passionless?—no, yet free from guilt or pain,
Which were, for his will made or suffered them,
Nor yet exempt, though ruling them like slaves,
From chance, and death, and mutability,
The clogs of that which else might oversoar
The loftiest star of unascended heaven,
Pinnacled dim in the intense inane.

PERCY BYSSHE SHELLEY, *Prometheus Unbound*, Act III (1820)

WRITINGS AGAINST GODWIN

DIALOGUE IN THE SHADES

Lucian. You appear very melancholy, for a philosopher of
the new stoical sect. Do you regret the glory, which you

doubtless enjoyed in the other world? Or do you dislike the grim equality of the stalking skeletons which surround you? We cannot boast, indeed, of our gaiety, but we have tranquillity, which, to a philosopher, is much better. We enjoy our exemption from the perturbations of life, as the wearied mariner reposes in the still gloom, succeeding a mighty tempest.

Neodidactus. Enjoy yourselves as you will; I am tormented by anxiety and doubt. By professing the doctrines of the new and pure philosophy on earth, my character was ruined, and I was abandoned by society. Here, I find no-one disposed to investigate my principles, excepting yourself, who, I suppose, intend to laugh at me, according to your custom. I had learned indeed from our master, that "the wise man is satisfied with nothing"; that "he is not satisfied with his own attainments or even with his principles and opinions"; but I feel that mine have produced the extremity of wretchedness.

Lucian. You must then be extremely wise, on your own principles. But be not dejected. The world, I perceive, preserves its old character; mankind have seldom troubled their benefactors with expressions of gratitude.

Neodidactus. I beg that you may never again mention so disagreeable a word to me. Gratitude, according to the new philosophy 'is no part either of justice or virtue'; nay, we hold it to be actually a vice when it results merely from our sense of benefits conferred on us.

Lucian. By the Graces! this is very strange philosophy. In teaching men to be ungrateful do you not render them wicked?

Neodidactus. We do not embarrass ourselves much with the distinctions of virtue and vice; the motives and tendencies of human actions are so complex, and their results so uncertain, that we find it difficult to assign them places under those designations. We even doubt whether there be any such thing as vice.

Lucian. You puzzle me; let me beg that you would explain yourself a little more clearly; unless your philosophy enjoins you to be obscure.

Neodidactus. I will explain myself most gladly. Know then, that "vice, as it is most commonly understood, is, so far as regards the motive, purely negative" and that "actions in the highest degree injurious to the public have often proceeded from motives uncommonly conscientious. The most determined political assassins, Clement, Ravaillac, Damiens and Gerard, seem to have been deeply penetrated with anxiety for the eternal welfare of mankind." Our sublime contemplations lead us also to believe, that "benevolence probably had its part in lighting the fires of Smithfield, and pointing the daggers of St Bartholomew."

Lucian. If I rightly understand you, murder and persecution are justifiable on the principles of the new philosophy.

Neodidactus. Our only rule is the promotion of general good by strict, impartial justice; whatever inconveniences may arise to individuals from this system, we disregard them, and as we allow no merit to actions which respect the good of individuals only, so we perceive no demerit in those which benefit the public, though they may considerably injure individuals. Justice, eternal justice must prevail.

Lucian. But how shall this over-ruling justice be ascertained or limited? If every man is to decide for himself and the world, confusion and universal ruin must ensue.

Neodidactus. You speak, O Lucian, of man in his present state; but we regard him in the state of perfection, to which he may attain by instructions and experience. We hope the time may arrive when neither government nor laws will be necessary to the existence of society; for morality is nothing but the probable advantages, or rather disadvantages, of our actions.

Lucian. By what means then shall those be corrected, who may err in their calculations respecting the public good, and eternal justice? For, I suppose, you can hardly expect that all men will reason with equal acuteness, in the most enlightened periods.

Neodidactus. By persuasion; the only allowable method of suppressing human errors. The establishment of positive laws is an insult to the dignity of man; so greatly do we detest their influence that we consider an honest lawyer as a worse member of society than a dishonest one, because the man of integrity palliates, and in some degree masks, the ill effects of law.

Lucian. This part of your philosophy is not so new as you imagine. All punishments, then, would be banished from your republic, excepting the long discourses to which you would oblige criminals to listen.

Neodidactus. Punishment is nothing else than force, and he who suffers it must be debased, and insensible of the difference between right and wrong, if he does not consider it as unjust. "I have deeply reflected, suppose, upon the nature of virtue, and am convinced that a certain proceeding is incumbent on me. But the hangman, supported by an Act of Parliament, assures me that I am mistaken." Can anything be more atrocious? more injurious to our sublime speculations?

Lucian. Doubtless, philosophers of your sect must sometimes be disagreeably interrupted, in their progress towards perfection. But in a society without laws, without the fear of the fear of punishment for offences, without the distinctions of virtue and vice, and destitute of the ties of gratitude and friendship, I feel it difficult to conceive, how the transactions necessary to existence can be carried on. You must depend much on family attachments, and on the inviolable regard which individuals should pay to their promises.

Neodidactus. Family attachments we regard as silly, and even criminal when they tend to bias our opinions; and as to promises, our master has written a long chapter to prove that they are great evils, and are only to be observed when we find it convenient.

Lucian. Did it never occur to you that this system might produce more evil than good in the world? and that you have been recommending a plan, which, instead of perfecting man, and improving society, must be destructive of every estimable quality in his breast, and must drive him again into savage solitude?

Neodidactus. We cannot always answer for events. "Everything is connected in the universe. If any man asserted that, if Alexander had not bathed himself in the river Cydnus, Shakespeare would never have written, it would be impossible to affirm that his assertion was untrue." Such is our doctrine.

Lucian. Your logic is equally admirable with your morality, this species of sophism has been exploded with contempt by good authors; you now revive it as one of your discoveries, and you may, perhaps, raise it to the rank of those which merit indignation. . . . But come, that we may part in good humour, I will treat you with a sentiment, which I derive from a dear friend of Swift. "We are for a just partition of the world, for every man has a right to enjoy life. We retrench the superfluities of mankind. The world is avaricious, and we hate avarice. A covetous fellow, like a jackdaw, steals what he was never made to enjoy, for the sake of hiding it. These are the robbers of mankind, for money was made for the free-hearted and generous; and where is the injury of taking from another what he has not the heart to make use of?" What is your opinion of this?

Neodidactus. It is admirably expressed, in the true spirit of our philosophy, and of impartial justice. Indeed, our master has said something very like it. Pray, in what divine work is this great truth to be found?

Lucian. In the *Beggar's Opera*; it expresses the sentiments of a gang of highwaymen, an institution which approaches nearer to your idea of perfect society, than any other with which I am acquainted.

The Anti-Jacobin Review (June 1799)

FROM "THE VISION OF LIBERTY"

Then saw I mounted on a braying ass
William and Mary, sooth, a couple jolly;
Who married, note ye how it came to pass,
Although each held that marriage was but folly?
And she of curses would discharge a volley
If the ass stumbled, leaping pales or ditches:
Her husband, sans-culottes, was melancholy,
For Mary verily would wear the breeches—
God help poor silly men from such usurping b——s.

Whilom this dame the *Rights of Women* writ,
That is the title to her book she places,
Exhorting bashful womankind to quit
All foolish modesty and coy grimaces;
And name their backsides as it were their faces;
Such licence loose-tongued liberty adores,
Which adds to female speech exceeding graces;
Lucky the maid that on her volume pores,
A scripture, archly fram'd for propagating w——s.

William hath penn'd a wagon-load of stuff,
And Mary's life at last he needs must write,
Thinking her whoredoms were not known enough,
Till printed off in black and white.—
With wondrous glee and pride, this simple wight
Her brothel feats of wantonness sets down,
Being her spouse, he tells, with huge delight,
How oft she cuckolded the silly clown,
And lent, O lovely piece! herself to half the town.

                    The Anti-Jacobin Review (August 1801)

NAKED REASON

This was the time when all things tending fast
To depravation, the Philosophy
That promised to abstract the hopes of man
Out of his feelings, to be fix'd thenceforth
For ever in a purer element
Found ready welcome. Tempting region that
Where passions had the privilege to work
And never hear the sound of their own names;
But, speaking more in charity, the dream
Was flattering to the young ingenuous mind
Pleas'd with extremes, and not the least with that
Which makes the human Reason's naked self
The object of its fervour. What delight!
How glorious! in self-knowledge and self-rule,
To look through all the frailties of the world,
And, with a resolute mastery shaking off
The accidents of nature, time and place,
That make up the weak being of the past,
Build social freedom on its only basis,
The freedom of the individual mind,
Which, to the blind restraint of general laws
Superior, magisterially adopts
One guide, the light of circumstances, flash'd
Upon an independent intellect.

WILLIAM WORDSWORTH, *The Prelude*, Book X, *ll.* 806–830
(1805)

Compare Oswald's speech in *The Borderers* (1796–97), Act III:

THE ONLY LAW

. . . I feel
That you have shown, and by a signal instance,
How they who would be just must seek the rule

By diving for it into their own bosoms.
To-day you have thrown off a tyranny[1]
That lives but in the torpid acquiescence
Of our emasculated souls, the tyranny
of the world's masters, with the musty rules
By which they uphold their craft from age to age:
You have obeyed the only law that sense
Submits to recognize; the immediate law,
From the clear light of circumstances, flashed
Upon an Independent intellect.

WILLIAM WORDSWORTH, *The Borderers*, Act III (1796)

PERFECTIBILITY

Mr Foster, who, we must observe, was a thin gentleman, about thirty years of age, with an aquiline nose, black eyes, white teeth and black hair—took occasion to panegyrise the vehicle in which they were then travelling, and observed what remarkable improvements had been made in the means of facilitating intercourse between distant parts of the kingdom: he held forth with great energy on the subject of roads and railways, canals and tunnels, manufacturers and machinery: "In short" said he, "everything we look on attests the progress of mankind in all the arts of life, and demonstrates their gradual advancement towards a state of unlimited perfection."

Mr Escot, who was somewhat younger than Mr Foster, but rather more pale and saturnine in his aspect, here took up the thread of the discourse, observing that the proposition just advanced seemed to him perfectly contrary to the true state of the case: "for" said he, "these improvements, as you call them, appear to me only so many links in the great chain of corruption, which will soon fetter the whole human race in irreparable slavery and incurable wretchedness: your improvements proceed in a simple ratio, while the factitious wants and

---

[1] *I.e.*, by committing murder.

unnatural appetites they engender proceed in a compound one; and thus one generation acquires fifty wants, and fifty means of supplying them are invented, which each in its turn engenders two new ones; so that the next generation has a hundred, the next two hundred, the next four hundred, till every human being becomes such a compound of perverted inclinations, that he is altogether at the mercy of external circumstances, loses all independence and singleness of character, and degenerates so rapidly from the primitive dignity of his sylvan origin, that it is scarcely possible to indulge in any other expectation, than that the whole species must at length be exterminated by its own infantine imbecility and vileness."

"Your opinions" said Mr Jenkinson, a round-faced little gentleman of about forty-five, "seem to differ *toto cælo*. I have often debated the matter in my own mind, pro and con, and have at length arrived at this conclusion—that there is not in the human race either a tendency to moral perfectibility or deterioration; but that the quantities of each are so exactly balanced by their reciprocal results, that the species, with respect to the sum of good and evil, knowledge and ignorance, happiness and misery, remains exactly and perpetually in *status quo*.

"Surely" said Mr Foster, "you cannot maintain such a proposition in face of evidence so luminous. Look at the progress of all the arts and sciences—see chemistry, botany, astronomy ——"

"Surely" said Mr Escot, "experience deposes against you. Look at the rapid growth of corruption, luxury, selfishness ——"

"Really, gentlemen" said the Reverend Doctor Gaster, after clearing the husk in his throat with two or three hems, "this is a very sceptical, and, I must say, atheistical conversation, and I should have thought, out of respect to my cloth ——"

Here the coach stopped, and the coachman, opening the

door, vociferated—"Breakfast gentlemen"; a sound which so gladdened the ears of the divine, that the alacrity with which he sprang from the vehicle superinduced a distortion of his ankle, and he was obliged to limp into the inn between Mr Escot and Mr Jenkinson; the former observing that he ought to look for nothing but evil, and, therefore, should not be surprised at this little accident; the latter remarking, that the comfort of a good breakfast, and the pain of a sprained ankle, pretty exactly balanced each other.

THOMAS LOVE PEACOCK, *Headlong Hall*, Chapter I (1816)

CHRONOLOGICAL TABLES

(a) LIFE OF GODWIN

1756. William Godwin born at Wisbech. Father a Dissenting minister.

1764. Sent to the school of Robert Akers at Hindolveston.

1767. Went as pupil to Samuel Newton, Independent minister at Norwich.

1773–77. Attended the Hoxton Academy of Dr Kippis.

1778. Became minister at Ware, in Hertfordshire.

1783. Minister at Beaconsfield till setting up as author. (For record of publications see Bibliography.)

1796. Met Mary Wollstonecraft.

1797. (March 29). Married in Old St Pancras Church.

1797. (August 30). Daughter, Mary, born. The mother died of a fever.

1801. Married Mrs Clairmont.

1805. Opened publishing business.

1812. Was written to by Shelley in January, and met him in London during October.

1812. Shelley eloped with Mary Godwin.

1816. Fanny Imlay (a daughter born to Mary Wollstonecraft before she met Godwin) poisoned herself at Swansea. Harriet, Shelley's wife, drowned herself on being deserted by her lover, and Shelley married Mary Godwin.

1822. Godwin became bankrupt. Rescued by friends.

1833. Whig Government under Lord Grey gave Godwin post of Yeoman Usher of the Exchequer.

1836. Died.

(b) HISTORICAL BACKGROUND

1760–1820. Reign of George III

1760–82. Government of the 'King's Friends.'

1783–1801. Government of Younger Pitt and the New Tories.
1775–82. American War.
1789–93. French Revolution.
1792–1802. War with France.
1794. *Habeas Corpus* repealed.
1799–1800. Combination Acts passed.

1811–20. The Regency.

1801–15. Group system of Tories and Whig Remnant.
1803–15. War with France.
1815. Corn Laws passed.
1817–19. Further repressive measures added to those of the seventeen-nineties.

1820–30. Reign of George IV.

1815–30. Tory Government of Liverpool, Wellington, and Peel.
1823. Repeal of Combination Acts.
1825. Tariff Reform.
1828. Test and Corporation Acts repealed.
1832. First Reform Bill.

NOTES

All the major difficulties of the Text are elucidated in the Introduction. These Notes are intended to cover minor difficulties, and those points of reference or interest that are not self-explanatory, in both Text and Introduction.

p. 36. *Fénelon*. François de Salignac de la Mothe Fénelon (1651–1715). The "illustrious archbishop of Cambray" referred to on p. 106. Appointed preceptor to the grandson of Louis XIV in 1689, he wrote several pedagogic works for his royal pupil. The most famous of these, the *Aventures de Télémaque* (1699), combined romance with moral teaching and instruction in Greek mythology and antiquities. Its politics were Utopian, and it was sufficiently satirical to arouse the anger of the King when (clandestinely) published.

p. 38. "*Dr Parr's Spital Sermon*." Samuel Parr (1747–1825), 'the Whig Johnson,' was noted as a pedagogue, a political writer, and a supporter of Godwin. But on April 15, 1800, having become estranged by Godwin's strictures on the clergy in *The Enquirer*, he took the opportunity presented by his being asked to deliver the annual Spital Sermon before the Lord Mayor to make a full-scale attack on Godwinism.

p. 40. *Holcroft*. Thomas Holcroft (1745–1809). Beginning as a stable-boy, Holcroft became in turn shoemaker, tutor, actor, and successful dramatist. In 1784 he played Figaro at Covent Garden in his own translation of *Le Mariage de Figaro*, which he had memorized by attending performances in Paris. He remained to the end a Radical and a close friend of Godwin.

p. 40. *Mackintosh*. Sir James Mackintosh (1765–1832), philosopher and barrister. In 1791 he published *Vindiciæ Gallicæ*, in reply to Burke's *Reflections on the French Revolution* (1790). However, on becoming known to Burke he changed his views, and, between January and June 1799, gave a series of public lectures *On the Law of Nature and Nations*, intended "publicly and unequivocally to abhor, abjure, and for ever renounce the French Revolution, with all its sanguinary history, its abominable principles, and for ever execrable leaders." His abhorrence apparently extended to all the progressive writers of the time, including his formerly admired friend Godwin. Hazlitt wrote:

> Poor Godwin, who had come, in the *bonhomie* and candour of his nature, to hear what new light had broken in upon his old friend, was obliged to quit the field, and slank away after an exulting taunt thrown out at "such fanciful chimeras as a golden mountain or a perfect man."

p. 43. *Burke—then a conservative, but, none the less, significantly admired by Godwin.* Godwin's attitude, and his manner of applying his philosophy, are well illustrated by the footnote added to Book VIII, Chapter Ten, of the third edition, when he heard the news of Burke's death (1797):

> In all that is most exalted in talents, I regard him as the inferior of no man that ever adorned the face of the earth; and, in the long record of human genius, I can find for him very few equals. In subtlety of discrimination, in magnitude of conception, in sagacity and profoundness of judgement, he was never surpassed. But his characteristic excellencies were vividness and justness of painting, and that boundless wealth of imagination that adorned the most ungrateful subjects, and heightened the most interesting. Of this wealth he was too lavish; and, though it is impossible for the man of taste not to derive gratification from almost every one of his images and metaphors while it passes before him, yet their exuberance subtracts, in no inconsiderable degree, from that irresistibleness and rapidity of general effect, which is the highest excellence of composition. No impartial man can recal Burke to his mind, without confessing the grandeur and integrity of his feelings of morality, and being convinced that he was eminently both the patriot and the philanthropist. His excellencies however were somewhat tinctured with a vein of dark and saturnine temper; so that the same man strangely united a degree of the rural character of his native island, with an urbanity and susceptibility of the kinder affections that have rarely been paralleled. But his principal defect consisted in this: that the false estimate as to the things entitled to our deference and admiration, which alone could render the aristocracy, with whom he lived, unjust to his worth, in some degree infected his own mind. He therefore sought wealth and plunged into expence, instead of cultivating the simplicity of indepen-

dence; and he entangled himself with a petty combination of
political men, instead of reserving his illustrious talents
unwarped for the advancement of intellect and the service
of mankind. He has unfortunately left us a memorable example
of the power of a corrupt system of government to undermine
and divert from their genuine purposes the noblest faculties
that have yet been exhibited to the observation of the world.

p. 46. *Shelley's transition from the revolutionary materialism of "Queen
Mab."* Like the statement on p. 15, attributing to the different
Romantic poets metaphysical, political, *or* literary theories, this
is, of course, an over-simplification. Shelley, like the other
Romantics, was concerned from beginning to end with both
idealist and materialist metaphysics, as well as with political and
literary theory. The change in Shelley's outlook—like the
theoretic differences between the Romantics—is a matter of
degree, not kind.

p. 48. *Shelley . . . conception of Nature.* This was never entirely
consistent or clear. But the conception may be somewhat
clarified if we consider it to be based—as it seems to be—on a
half-conscious analogy of *Nature* with a human being, in whom
the mind may be thought to work through and guide, a body
which—though not separable from the mind—is yet subject to
physical laws. This would account for the belief, expressed in
Queen Mab, that all matter is alive and feeling, and for the conception of mind as a sort of electricity, material enough to persist
after death as part of the "collective energy of the moral and
material world." Behind this, no doubt, lies the neo-Platonic
spiritus mundi and the similar Oriental conceptions which affected
Shelley's Platonism.

p. 70. *Man did not enter into society to become worse.* Paine here
accepts the 'social contract' theory of the origin of government,
expounded—with considerable difference of emphasis—in
Hobbes's *Leviathan* (1651) and Locke's second *Treatise on Government* (1690). According to this 'pre-evolutionary' theory, men
deliberately surrendered the freedoms of the state of nature in
exchange for the security of a state of society.

p. 92. *. . . unfold his stores.* The 'jargon' Godwin refers to is, of
course, that of Plato (see the *Meno*).

p. 98. *We cannot discover the causes of things.* Godwin derives his
doctrine from Hume, who first subjected the concept of causality
to logical analysis (see the *Treatise of Human Nature* (1739),

Book I, Part 3, or—for a brief summary of his conclusions—
An Enquiry concerning Human Understanding (1748), Section VII,
Part 2).

p. 136. *This has been too much the case with the teachers of religion, even
those of them who are most eager in their hostility to religious enthusiasm.*
The 'even' is presumably prompted by the tendency of the
Enthusiasts to elevate Grace above Works (*cf.* p. 143 ... *according
to the system of certain religionists, "he may live as he list, for he cannot
commit sin."*)

p. 141. *optimism.* The doctrine developed by Leibniz (1646–1716)
from the combined postulates of omnipotence and complete benevolence, and epitomized by Pope in the phrase, "whatever is,
is right." The most notable satire on the doctrine is Voltaire's
Candide (1759). (*Cf.* footnote at p. 23.)

SELECT BIBLIOGRAPHY

Background

TURBERVILLE, A. S. (editor): *Johnson's England* (Oxford, two vols., 1933).

GEORGE, M. D.: *London Life in the Eighteenth Century* (London, 1925). *England in Transition* (London, 1931).

HALÉVY, E.: *History of the English People in the Nineteenth Century* (London, 1924).

HAZLITT, W.: *The Spirit of the Age* (London, 1825).

HUGHES, A. M. D.: *The Nascent Mind of Shelley* (Chapter X), (Oxford, 1947).

STEPHEN, L.: *History of English Thought in the Eighteenth Century* (London, 1876).

TOYNBEE, A.: *Lectures on the Industrial Revolution* (London, 1884).

TREVELYAN, G. M.: *English Social History* (London, 1944).

WILLEY, B.: *The Eighteenth-century Background* (London, 1940).

Godwin

BRAILSFORD, H. N.: *Shelley, Godwin, and their Circle* (London, 1914).

GODWIN, W.: *The Life of Chatham* (1783).

An Account of the Seminary that will be opened on Monday the Fourth Day of August at Epsom in Surrey (1783).

The Herald of Literature (1784).

Sketches of History, in Six Sermons (1784).

An Enquiry concerning the Principles of Political Justice, and its Influence on General Virtue and Happiness (two vols., 1793). Second edition (two vols., 1796). Third edition (two vols., 1798).

There are also more recent editions of *Political Justice*, edited by F. E. L. Priestley (Toronto, three vols., 1946), and A. A. Knopf (New York, abridged, 1926).

Things as they are; or the Adventures of Caleb Williams (1794)
(Reprinted, Newnes, 1904).

*Cursory Strictures on Lord Chief Justice Eyre's Charge to the Grand
Jury* (1794) (Anon.).

Considerations on Lord Grenville's and Mr Pitt's Bills (1795) (by
'A Lover of Order').

The Enquirer: Reflection on Education (1797).

Manners and Literature (1797).

Memoirs of the Author of the Rights of Woman (1798) (Reprinted,
Constable, 1928).

St Leon (1799).

Antonio: a Tragedy in Five Acts (1800).

Thoughts Occasioned by Dr Parr's Spital Sermon, etc. (1801).

The Life of Geoffrey Chaucer (1803).

Fleetwood: or The New Man of Feeling (1805).

Fables, Ancient and Modern (1805).

The Looking Glass: a True History of the Early Years of an Artist
(1805).

The Pantheon: or the Ancient History of the Gods of Greece and Rome
(1806).

The History of England (1806).

The Life of Lady Jane Grey, and of Guildford Dudley, her Husband
(1806).

Faulkener; a Tragedy (1807).

The History of Rome (1809).

A New Guide to the English Tongue (1809).

An Essay on Sepulchres (1809).

The Lives of Edward and John Phillips, Nephews and Pupils of Milton
(1809).

The History of Greece (1811).

Mandeville: A Tale of the Seventeenth Century (1817).

*Of Population: an Enquiry concerning the Power of Increase in the
Numbers of Mankind; being an Answer to Mr Malthus's Essay*
(1820).

*History of the Commonwealth of England, from its Commencement
to the Restoration of Charles the Second* (four vols., 1824–28).

Cloudesley (1830).

Thoughts on Man, his Nature, Productions and Discoveries (1831).

Deloraine (1833).

The Lives of the Necromancers; or, An Account of the Most Eminent Persons in Successive Ages, who have claimed for themselves, or to whom has been imputed to them by others, the Exercise of Magical Power (1834).

Essays (1873).

(The above list contains all Godwin's surviving works.)

INGPEN (editor): *The Love Letters of Mary Wollstonecraft* (London, 1908).

KEGAN, PAUL: *William Godwin: His Friends and Contemporaries* (London, 1876).

WOODCOCK, G.: *William Godwin* (London, 1946).